KEN DICK, CA

WHAT ARE YOU DOING WITH MY MONEY?

Solutions to important issues facing charities

Ken Dick Management Consultants
P.O. Box 202, Streetsville, Ontario, Canada, L5M 2B8

Copyright by Ken Dick ©

ISBN 0-9695560-0-4

Cover illustration by: David Bathurst

Published by: Ken Dick Management Consultants
P.O. Box 202, Streetsville, Ontario L5M 2B8

Printed in Canada by: Harmony Printing Limited, 123 Eastside Drive,
Toronto, Ontario

DEDICATION

To my wife Marlene, my greatest encourager,

and to the memory of my father, Walter,

who taught me that there is

something to like in everybody.

Contents

Introduction

When I resigned from World Vision in June 1990 the marketing department produced a video for my farewell party. It featured a camera crew searching the building looking for Ken Dick. Several staff were asked if they knew Ken Dick but nobody had heard of me and Personnel had no record of me. After much searching, my name was finally discovered on the door of a room containing janitorial supplies. The President was then interviewed and it was established that Ken Dick did work at World Vision and had done so for the past 15 years. Perhaps the camera crew should also have asked, "What did Ken Dick learn while he was there and what did he contribute?"

This book answers that question by looking at what I have learned during more than 25 years in Administration and Management.

Is this just another book on management? Not really. The difference between this book and other books written on the subject is that this book looks at managing a unique type of enterprise. Over half of my own experience in management has been gained from working with non-profit organizations and most of this book looks at managing within that context.

But it is not only about managing non-profits. Principles that I have learned, tried and sometimes discarded, can be used by managers in any type of organization.

This book contains my experiences in managing and what I learned from them. It is not a technical book. It looks at the lessons I have learned from the battles managers find themselves in every day.

Student-in-Accounts

My battle began in the charming town of Orillia which Stephen Leacock popularized in the book Sunshine Sketches. When my wife and I arrived in Orillia in the summer of 1960 with our baby daughter, we walked into the pages of Leacock's book. Neither of us had ever been this far away from family and friends, but we willingly accepted my company's request to transfer to their Orillia office. Eddis & Associates, Chartered Accountants, had employed me during the summer of 1957 with the understanding that I return to article with them the following year after graduating from York Memorial Collegiate. Having now spent a year in their Toronto office as a 'student-in-accounts', they offered me the opportunity to work in a much different environment in Orillia.

Being involved with small business clients interested me. In Toronto, my work had exposed me to mostly large companies such as Drug Trading (I.D.A.), Toronto Carpet, Supreme Aluminum, and Toronto Western Hospital. In Orillia there were not many large companies. At that time the town proudly promoted itself as a small community of 15,000 people, which tripled in size during the summers when cottagers and boaters arrived. This was to be my working environment for the next three years.

The weeks flew by as I threw myself into the work and my studies. Three, and sometimes four nights each week were spent completing lessons in law, accounting and auditing, for submission to Queens University. This ritual involved taking over the kitchen in our small flat by relegating my wife, Marlene, and our growing family of two babies to the living room. Marlene was my greatest supporter, especially during those times when I felt like finding a job that would pay more. But I had to be reminded that certain sacrifices had to be made if I were to reach my goal of becoming a CA.

Any time I doubted my decision I remembered a confrontation with my public school principal when I was in grade eight.

"Why did you light that match in the classroom, Ken? You know it's against school regulations. You should know better at your age".

Mr. Wilcox's voice droned on ... "What are you going to do with your life? You've got potential. You're a good student. What do you want to be ... a lawyer ... a doctor ... a ...?"

Before he completed the question, I blurted out, "A chartered accountant sir". I don't know why I said it. I didn't know any chartered accountants. In fact, I wasn't even sure what they did! But as I entered into my first year at high school, that was my career goal – and it never changed.

Into the Business World

It had never been my intention to remain in public accounting after I became a CA. A partnership in the Eddis firm was a distinct possibility, especially if I had remained in Orillia. But I never saw my career in that arena. I wanted to get into the business world.

One of my clients, Commercial Caterers Limited, was the type of company that interested me. It was privately owned and small enough that management staff were involved in all aspects of the operation. I remember coming home and saying to Marlene, "The office manager at Commercial has exactly the type of job I want. He is involved in all aspects of the business, including personnel". Within weeks of making that statement, I was being interviewed for his job! He had resigned and I had been asked to consider the position. In January 1964, Commercial Caterers Limited had a new office manager. The company, founded in 1948, was owned by Art Young, Alf Martin and Leo Irwin. My responsibilities could have been stated in one sentence, "Look after the finances and keep us out of trouble". During the next two years I attempted to do just that, while at the same time major events were changing the face of the company. With the deaths of Alf and Art, Leo found himself in the unenviable position of attempting to manage the company on his own. During 1965, Claude Switzer, the sales manager and I found ourselves meeting with Leo as a management team. One day he dropped a 'bombshell' on us. "How would you like to buy this company?"

My heart pounded with excitement for about one minute until the price tag of over a quarter million dollars made me consider the fact that I was a recent CA graduate with a wife, three children and no money! It could never be done. Leo went on to explain how we could come up with the money over the next three years by using the company's own reserves. Within two years of joining the company I became Secretary-Treasurer with a 50% ownership. The scope of my responsibilities increased considerably. Along with administrative and financial functions, my workload suddenly included contract negotiations and public relations activities with our many clients. I couldn't believe that at age 27 I would be successfully negotiating a contract to operate the concessions and banquet services in the new Toronto O'Keefe Centre. That was just the beginning as we continued to service new facilities, including the Medical Arts Building at the University of Toronto, the Cummer Home for the Aged in Toronto and a duty-free store at the airport in Gander, Newfoundland.

From 1966 until 1972 I was involved in every aspect of business activity. It was a wonderful opportunity for me to learn the art of managing. As an owner, the responsibility for anything that happened ultimately fell on my partner and me.

Filling in for sick staff one day, I found myself serving soup on the cafeteria line at one of our locations in the University of Toronto. Negotiating contracts with our unionized staff in Newfoundland in a smoke-filled hotel room was another experience in my early management career. Then there was the difficult period when the bank wouldn't extend additional credit to us and we had to keep the creditors 'at bay' while scratching for funds to pay our staff. At one point I faced the possibility of losing everything – business and personal assets. However, as the economy improved the business improved and the future began to look more positive.

Lessons learned during eight years in my own business would prove to be invaluable in the years to come. I knew that part of the company's success had been due to my participation in its management. When I left in 1972, we had 250 staff and revenues exceeding $4 million.

Having relinquished my ownership in the company, I moved into a management position with Nestle (Canada) Limited, as Manager, Financial Control.

The Multi National Corporation

The transition from a small private company to a large conglomerate with operations in nearly every country of the world and revenue in the billions of dollars was traumatic, to say the least. The children were excited – they could only see the immediate benefits to the family – a never-ending supply of Quik, Nestle's famous chocolate drink. My reaction to this major career move went deeper than Nestle's product line. After 8 years in business, I was no longer my own boss!

With a staff of twenty-five in my department, I began to experience new adventures in management, many of them unique to a large corporation. The scope of my responsibilities included Accounts Payable, Accounts Receivable, Inventory Control, General Ledger and financial statement preparation, along with bank and cash control functions and foreign currency transactions. 'Challenging' and 'growth' are the words which best describe the three years I spent with the Nestle company.

One thing I appreciated about Nestle – they valued their staff and whenever possible, promoted from within. Don McCarthy, the President at the time, had worked in the Toronto office for several years and had come up through the ranks. My own career path, according to my superiors, would eventually place me in the position of Vice-President, Finance. That was my goal, and it would be attainable within five years when the incumbent retired. Such a move would be preceded by eight months in Switzerland attending the Nestle sponsored business management school.

But I had no idea that a visit to Toronto by the World Vision Korean Childrens Choir in the late sixties would have a profound impact on my career. Our family became sponsors of a Korean orphan named Joo Hyun.

Through a series of events and meetings with this world-wide Christian charity I became a volunteer, serving on the Canadian Investment Committee. I enjoyed my part-time involvement with this organization while pursuing my career goals at Nestle.

In early 1974 the telephone rang in my office. It was Ian, one of the World Vision management staff who served with me on the Investment Committee.

"Ken", he started. "World Vision has a problem. With the rapid growth in income we need a senior financial person to work with us. Possibly someone with an accounting degree. Would you know of anyone"?

I told him I would let him know if anyone came to mind.

Several months later a second, more serious call came from Ian.

"Things are getting worse. We really need help. Don't you know any CAs that might work with us"?

My response was similar to what I had said several months before. "No names come to mind but I will give it some thought".

Then he responded with what I thought was a most ridiculous comment, but one that would eventually change the direction of my life.

"WHAT ABOUT YOU"?

I remember laughing and responding with some off-handed comment, "you can't afford me". Although said in jest as I sat with my feet on the desk, visions of a wonderful future with Nestles flashed through my mind. Ridiculous to even think that I would give up all of this to work for a charity.

"Would you at least have lunch with the Treasurer of the board"?

My next words would come back to haunt me for years, "no harm in talking".

The rest is history.

Are We Missionaries, Daddy?

These were the words that greeted my announcement to the family that daddy was going to work for a charitable organization. Perhaps it was the World Vision mailer with my picture on it that prompted Karen, our oldest daughter, to ask the question. After all, we did have pictures of other missionaries on our kitchen bulletin board.

No, I was not a missionary – at least not in the truest sense of the word. World Vision Canada is a Christian humanitarian agency, incorporated and registered with Revenue Canada as a charitable organization. All staff are paid a salary.

The impact of my move to the world of charities was felt immediately in several areas, but mainly in size and goals. In 1975 World Vision was housed in 11,000 square feet of crowded space in north-east Toronto, a far cry from the Nestle building and with considerably fewer staff and less income. The goals were to raise funds to assist needy people, quite different from the need to make a profit for shareholders.

Over the next fifteen years, I saw the organization grow and change in many different ways. In 1975 their accounting records were maintained manually. When I resigned in 1990 we had just signed a contract with IBM for the installation of a new AS400 main frame computer, one of three in-house systems. But computerization was only one major area of change in my responsibilities. During my time with World Vision the organization moved into a new building in Mississauga and its annual income grew from $4 million to over $60 million.

I travelled to other parts of the world as I became more involved in financial management matters and internal audits for World Vision International. Worldwide, the organization raises over $300 million (U.S.) and supports approximately one million children through its sponsorship program. As Acting Vice-President, Finance for the International body for several months, I was involved in many other aspects of the operations of this humanitarian agency.

Leaving World Vision was something I never thought would happen, but in mid-1990 I resigned. After spending several months in Europe as a management consultant, I returned to Mississauga to become a consultant and practice as a Chartered Accountant.

Boards

During my years at World Vision, one of the most important lessons I learned was how boards and staff related to one another. (The first three chapters look at this important relationship, which causes a great deal of friction within many charitable organizations). During the past 25 years I have served on boards and had to report to boards. Elim Homes, a home for the aged in Ontario, was one of my first board appointments.

My work with World Vision was enhanced through 15 years of participation on the board of the Canadian Council of Christian Charities (CCCC), on which I still serve. It was interesting and challenging to be involved with them in the development of group insurance and pension plans, setting financial accountability standards, and laying a foundation for proper procedures for charities working with trust agreements. This group continues to dialogue with Revenue Canada on matters affecting charities.

Another "watchdog" of charities is the Toronto Better Business Bureau. My recent appointment to their Charities Review Board provides me with an opportunity to be part of a group which seeks to set fund raising standards by which charities will be evaluated and monitored.

I learned a lot during my 25 years in management. This book relates many of my experiences.

Walk with me through some of the joys, sorrows and disappoint-
ments that managers and board members experience.

1
Being on a Board Can be Fun – But Not Often

THE INVITATION

Why would anyone accept an invitation to serve on the board of a charitable organization? Prestige? Ego? Business contacts? Career advancement?

My first invitation came through a friend, as is so often the case. An innocent question, "Would you consider serving on the board of Elim Home? We need someone with a financial background".

"Well, I would want to know more about what's involved, and some time to think it over", was my initial response, not wanting to sound too excited or interested. Imagine, someone wants me to be on their board! Here I was, already into my thirties and no one had ever asked me to serve on a board. I was ready but didn't want to appear too anxious.

"When do you need to know, George?"

"We would like you to meet with our Treasurer and he can give you more detail and answer any questions you might have".

"Sounds good to me".

"He will call you".

He did call me a few days later and we met for lunch. (It's good to meet over lunch when dealing with important matters!)

"Ken, I've been with this board since its inception", said the Treasurer as we were being led to our table. "We need some new people, younger people like yourself on our board. We need someone who can help us in the financial areas. You know, some of the accounting, preparation of financial statements and things like that. I've been doing much of it myself for all of these years, but it's time that I hand over some of it to someone younger. Besides, my eyes are not what they used to be. At my age, things start to get a bit blurry. I feel I need to get away from the detail work".

The Treasurer was a delightful man, and quite elderly. I could not argue with his rationale.

He went on, "There's not a lot of work involved. We have a fairly small budget and only a few staff. We could use your help".

Like so many other charities, they needed some management expertise and hands-on support. It was twelve years after that meeting that I eventually resigned from that particular board.

There wasn't a lot of work involved. Just a few meetings each year. But the assistance they needed included all of the bookkeeping, preparation of annual financial statements, employee T4 slips and payment of accounts.

I'm not complaining. I knew what I was getting into. But, I soon realized what it meant to be a member of a working board. They not only set policy for the organization, but much of the administration falls on their shoulders as well. As is the case for most working boards, it's the financial areas that require the most help, especially in smaller charities.

Being a board member not only involves attending meetings and voting on issues, it may require many hours of voluntary activity outside of the board meetings in addition to your full time job and the responsibilities of being a husband and father.

In this chapter I am particularly concerned with looking through the eyes of board members. Having served for several years in a management role with a large charitable organization, I know the importance of understanding board members especially because of difficulties managers may experience relating to a board. Also, many managers are asked to serve on boards so it's important to examine the extent of that involvement. As a manager, you may also be asked to assist in establishing a board so it's a good idea to acquaint yourself with some of the dynamics involved when someone is considering a board appointment.

WHEN TO SAY YES AND WHEN TO SAY NO

Someone has been asked to serve on a board. There is nothing miraculous about making a decision. But most potential board members should ask themselves a few simple questions.

(a) Do I Have The Time?

If the answer is "no", then you need not bother asking yourself any further questions. This is the most important consideration. Once you have assessed the time commitment and decided you cannot give the time required, then say "no". I know too many people that serve on boards but cannot give the time required to contribute effectively. Or they give all the necessary time, but at the expense of other important activities in their lives. If you cannot meet the time commitment, do not accept the invitation. If joining the board means sacrificing time with your family, ask yourself what is more important to you (and to your family). Too often we hear the questioning wife (and sometimes the children) asking the board member husband/ father as he goes out the door, "Do you really have to go to another meeting tonight"?

If you have to take time away from your job in order to serve on a board, you had better be sure that your superiors know about it. Some employers are very supportive, but this may not always be the case.

To me, it's a simple matter of priorities. What are the most important things in your life? Can a board appointment be fitted into that list without sacrificing something else? Although it was not always the case, I now consider any invitation to serve on a board in relation to the time I can give. This kind of decision should also be discussed with one's spouse. It took me several years to realize that my wife often had better insight into this decision-making process than I did.

(b) Is The Organization One That I Can Support Unconditionally?

Board membership to me means commitment. Commitment to the organization, to its key objective, to its goals, to its people, to its raison d'être. A board member who is not totally committed to all of these things, should not be on the board! If you are on the board of an organization that you are not fully committed to, I suggest you resign. Non-committed board members can cause untold grief for an organization and its staff.

(c) What Can I Contribute?

I have been in board meetings where some board (bored?) members never utter a word. They even vote with their hands. Meeting after meeting, this is the pattern. They might ask the odd question, but often you can catch them dozing. They usually have to leave early, having arrived late. During a coffee break or a meal, they talk up a storm. When the meeting resumes, not a word.

Maybe I am being too cynical. But you have to ask yourself, "Why does he(*) even bother to come to the meeting?" Or perhaps a more important question, "Why is he even on the board?"

If you cannot contribute something meaningful to the organization, then do not accept an invitation in the first place. Make sure you ask those who extend the invitation, "What do you think I can contribute to the organization?"

HOW TO ACQUIRE QUALITY BOARD MEMBERS

Every charitable organization should use a Nominating Committee when searching for people to serve on its board. Most people recommended for board membership are suggested by someone already on the board or a staff member. There is nothing inherently wrong with this process if handled correctly, but unfortunate situations can occur if the nominations are not properly screened.

Nominating Committees

A Nominating Committee would normally consist of two or three members of the board and the organization's Chief Executive Officer (CEO). It would be responsible for screening all candidates and ultimately recommending to the board who should be considered for appointment. The screening process should be well organized and follow formal procedures. A two hour lunch with a candidate is not sufficient. A formal interview with a prepared list of questions should be conducted by the committee, either individually or as a group.

(*) For the sake of reading ease and continuity I have predominantly used the masculine pronoun. Feminine pronouns can easily be substituted whenever the masculine is used except in personal anecdotes.

All current board members should be given the names and background information on each candidate and asked for their input.

It is important to include the CEO on the Nominating Committee. Boards make policy but the CEO must adhere to these policies while providing leadership to the organization.

The CEO is expected to relate to every board member in some way because they are the people to whom he is ultimately responsible. Some of the problems between board members and CEOs could be avoided if the CEO is asked to give an opinion on board candidates. A lack of proper candidate screening can cause untold grief for a CEO and the organization.

The Nominating Committee should be unanimously agreed before proceeding with a candidate. A friend who was on a Nominating Committee resigned from an organization because of his strong feelings about a committee's recommendation. This is an unusual situation, but it does occur. It emphasizes the importance of complete unity on a committee's nominations. In this case, the opinion of the dissenting committee member proved to be correct. The committee's decision eventually became a source of grief to the organization for several years. Every committee should strive for unanimity. On boards where I have served, I have never been interviewed by a Nominating Committee or been asked to submit a personal profile. (Of course, I knew that the organizations would do some investigating of my background.) But it was not really proper for them to accept me based solely on a friend's recommendation. They knew about me, but they did not KNOW me!

References should be obtained from other boards on which the candidate serves or has served, and special attention should be paid to his previous performance. If nominating committees performed their mandates effectively, some people would never be elected to boards.

BOARD/STAFF RELATIONSHIPS
Dazzle

I pride myself in being able to get along with most people – even board members. When I joined World Vision I was young and more aggressive than I am now about many things, perhaps even to the point of being somewhat cocky. But this attribute was usually conveyed with a sense of humour.

Shortly after joining World Vision I attended an executive staff meeting. We were discussing the annual budget and how to present it to the board. There were some concerns about certain expense items and whether the board would approve them. How would we get them past those few board members who always made budget presentations difficult? Jokingly, I made the comment, "I'll dazzle them with my footwork". For the next several weeks the management team referred to me as DAZZLE. My children, having learned of my new nickname, presented me with a T-shirt for my birthday on which was emblazoned in large red letters the word DAZZLE.

At the next management team meeting I could not resist the temptation to further embarrass myself before my peers. Underneath my dress shirt I wore my DAZZLE shirt. At the appropriate time, while Bill Newell, the Executive Director was presenting his serious views on the budget, I rose from my seat. Turning my back to the group, I very nonchalantly removed my jacket and tie and unbuttoned my shirt. By this time all conversation had stopped. Everyone was looking at me.

Bill said, "What in the world are you doing"?

With that, I turned toward the group, pulled open my shirt and exposed the bright red lettering on my T-shirt while blurting out in a confident tone, "You don't have to worry about the board. I'll dazzle them with my footwork".

It took some time before the laughter subsided and we could return to the agenda.

I don't think I ever "dazzled" anyone, especially the board. What this incident accomplished though, was to introduce some humour into a serious discussion. There is a time for being serious, but management needs humour as well. I'm a firm believer in having fun in managing. This particular event followed me through almost 15 years in World Vision, and was even mentioned in the farewell event held in my honour.

Every management team would benefit by having a "dazzling" event once in awhile. Through the years I have attempted to introduce some humour into my board reports. Board meetings which are strictly business can lead to strained relationships. A little levity can alleviate some of this tension and lead to better relationships between board members and staff.

The Board And The CEO

One of the major reasons for conflict between board and staff hinges on the question, "Who is running this organization"?

The staff member most important to the board and the organization is the CEO. (The Chief Executive Officer could have the title of Executive Director or President, but we will use the term CEO to describe the person ultimately responsible for managing the organization.) The one problem that can destroy the effectiveness of an organization, demoralize its staff, lead to resignations of both board members and staff, and even result in legal problems, is the uncertainty of how a board should relate to the CEO.

The CEO is hired by and reports to the board through the board chairman. This does not mean that the CEO reports to the chairman. The board appoints the CEO, the chairman does not. The board can terminate the employment of the CEO, the chairman does not have this authority. The chairman's responsibilities include acting as a liaison between the board and management, and to provide support to the CEO as required and requested by the CEO.

It is not the responsibility of the chairman or any member of the board to do the job of the CEO! Support him – yes. Be there if he needs help – yes. Reprimand him if necessary – yes. But do not do his job for him. Meddling board members are the worst kind. Board members should always be very careful not to get involved in operational matters. (What constitutes an operational matter will be looked at in chapter three.)

The Importance Of Good Relationships

The CEO and the chairman must have a good relationship if the organization is going to effectively fulfil its goals. A poor relationship between these two positions will permeate the entire organization. The CEO's relationship with the chairman will determine how other staff members feel about him.

On one occasion, while serving as chairman of a board, I very innocently contacted an insurance broker in order to obtain some information which I thought would be of benefit to the organization. Shortly after, I received a long distance telephone call from another board member.

"Bill's nose is out of joint. He is quite upset with you, Ken".

He was speaking of the CEO.

"You must be kidding", I replied, What have I done?"

"Have you been obtaining information concerning insurance?"

"Yes, but I only made some inquiries", was my defensive response.

"Well, whatever you did, he thinks he should have been the one to do it. That's what we pay him for".

Needless to say, this situation upset me. The CEO and I were good friends. What I had failed to realize was the extent to which I was getting involved in what the CEO felt was an operational matter. I did it innocently and he may have overreacted. But nonetheless, it was something that he could have handled. I excused my actions by reminding him that the board had been very involved in operations when the organization was formed. The board had performed all the work because there hadn't been a CEO.

I failed to recognize that the CEO is responsible for operations and board members should only get involved at the request of the CEO. This was an important reminder for me. Too many board members delve into operational activities without being invited to do so.

A sensitive area? Definitely. One that should be clarified between the CEO and the board, leaving no room for situations to develop that will cause tension.

The Board And Staff

How should board members relate to staff? On what basis should board members have contact with staff on matters relating to operations? I am not referring to board members walking through the office and greeting staff, but to situations where board members go directly to staff for information without advising the CEO.

I worked for one CEO who made it very clear to the board and to his staff that no board/staff communication were to take place without his knowledge. He felt that the board should always obtain information through his office. This is one approach. This usually indicates that the CEO has had previous difficulties in this area. But it could also suggest that the CEO doesn't trust certain board members. Such a policy may also suggest that the CEO is insecure in his role. Few would disagree that a CEO should know what operational information is being fed to board members. But how this policy is implemented should be clearly understood.

There is one reasonable exception to this policy. The board's Treasurer should have direct access to the Chief Financial Officer. An understanding on this point should be established between the CEO, Treasurer and staff. The key to this procedure is to keep the CEO informed of any information staff members share with the board. No CEO wants surprises. To be confronted by a board member with information the CEO is unaware of is upsetting. It is the responsibility of the CEO to ensure that all staff understand how they should relate to board members and how to handle information requested by a board member.

One step in building good relationships between board and staff is to introduce board members to the staff. Employees in some organizations, many of whom have been with the organization for years, never meet or even know who is on the board! It is a good idea to have board members occasionally walk through the office and greet the staff. A staff meeting could also be arranged where one or more board members share their vision of the organization.

One of the international presidents of World Vision had attended board meetings in Canada many times over the years, but had never taken the time to meet staff members. Some employees wondered why they had never seen him. I mentioned this to him and on his next visit he made it a priority to walk through the office and greet the staff. They were pleased and encouraged by this gesture.

Regardless of the closeness that may exist between boards and staff, problems will arise. When they do, the board should deal with them immediately before they cause serious difficulties. A situation I was involved in as a staff member dragged on for several years. It never became an agenda item at any board meeting until it was too late. Any attempts to resolve the problem were by individuals outside of the formal board meetings. As a result, many board members were not even aware that there was a problem. I would not want to serve on a board where such a serious problem of interpersonal relationships existed and I wasn't informed of it. When a board becomes aware of a problem, they must get involved.

Relationship problems between board members and management not only can destroy the heart of an organization, they can be the greatest cause of both board and staff turnover.

Although we have been looking at the need to properly examine board candidates, we must also remember CEO candidates should also be screened. Problems of this nature are not always the fault of board members.

Another area of board/staff conflict is friction between the CEO and the board chairman. There are several ways this friction can be reduced.

Advice To The CEO

(a) Keep your board informed. They like to know what is happening to the organization for which they are ultimately responsible. They hired you to operate it, but they don't like surprises. Set up procedures whereby information will flow to them on a regular basis, not just on board meeting days.

(b) Meet with your board chairman regularly. He is your pipeline to the board. He should be a counsellor who you can go to with problems or to seek advice. Work at this relationship. It is important. If there are problems with the relationship, discuss it openly and work at resolving your differences. If they cannot be resolved, bring in someone to mediate. Do not let relational problems impair the effectiveness of the organization in meetings its goals.

(c) Help the board chairman plan board meetings, remembering it is a board meeting not a CEO meeting. Present items that you want to have on the agenda. Discuss them and attempt to obtain his support prior to the meeting. Having your chairman onside with you will assist you to achieve your own goals.

Advice To The Board Chairman

(a) Keep your CEO informed. He has been entrusted with the organization's operations. He is expected to be efficient. Anything that the board knows that will assist him in accomplishing this task should be shared with him.

(b) Meet with the CEO regularly. He needs your support. He needs to know that you care about him succeeding as the CEO. He needs to know that the board supports him. He needs to know if the board has any concerns about his leadership. Work at this relationship. Keep it open and do not let problems accumulate.

(c) Encourage exposure to senior staff at board meetings. It is meaningful to senior staff members to be invited to these meetings to give their reports. This should be done with the approval of the CEO. It is an excellent way for the board to meet senior management and for senior management to meet the policy makers.

2

True Love Never Runs Smooth: How to Keep the Board out of the Staff's Hair

There are a number of problems common to most boards, such as what do you do with troublesome board members and what role does a CEO have in setting up a board meeting?

Although solutions to these problems should be spelled out clearly in every organization, unfortunately this is not always the case. Consequently there are conflicts between board members themselves and between the board and staff.

Let's look at how conflicts develop before we consider some standard procedures that should be established to ensure board efficiency.

INEFFECTIVE AND TROUBLESOME BOARD MEMBERS

(a) The Non-Committed

"How long has he been a board member?"

"About five years".

"What does he think about the request for approving two million dollars for the new building?"

"I don't know".

"But it was discussed for two hours at the last meeting. Surely he had some opinion".

"I do remember him asking what time lunch was being served".

"Did he receive all of the materials on the project? They were sent out prior to the meeting".

"He said he had received them, but hadn't had time to read them".

"Well, how did he vote?"

"He didn't vote".

"What do you mean, he didn't vote?"

"He was on the telephone to his office when the vote was taken".

Sound familiar? The next question is obvious, "Why did he ever join the board?"

My analysis of the disinterested, non-committed board member has led me to conclude that they are on the board because they think their position gives them a certain status with friends and associates. They obtain some satisfaction, and in their minds a certain prestige, by being able to say to others that they are a member of a board. They might also feel some benefit is derived by including this information on their resumes in the hopes of obtaining some advantage when seeking employment.

Some boards have included a provision in their bylaws stating that missing three consecutive board meetings is grounds for being asked to resign. This rule helps to weed out the uncommitted.

(b) The Interrogator

On the other side of the coin there are those board members who ask too many questions. As the Chief Financial Officer of a charity I was often required to present financial information to the board. There are always plenty of questions when it come to finances. I didn't mind the questions but objected to a troublesome board member who asks the questions for the wrong reasons. Unlike the ineffective board member, this person never stops talking. You can be sure that at every meeting he will dominate parts of the discussion, if not a great deal of the overall meeting time. I have concluded that these members ask questions for one or more of the following reasons:

1. He is uninformed because he does not prepare for the meeting by reading the material sent to him in advance.

2. He wants to impress the other board members with his knowledge of the subject (but usually displays his lack of it).

3. He thinks the others will view him as a valuable and important member of the board because he has an interest in every agenda item.
4. He wants to embarrass the staff member to whom the questions are directed.
5. He wants the staff member to know who is really in charge.
6. He likes the sound of his own voice.

After being on the receiving end of many questions from board members over the years, I knew who would ask most of the questions at a meeting, how they would be phrased, and in what tone of voice they would be conveyed. Knowing this in advance really unnerved me. If I took 15 file folders of information with me into the meeting, you could be sure that the answer to at least one question would be in the folder left on my desk. I came out of many board meetings frustrated and angry, not so much because of the questions, but because of the way they were asked and why they had been asked.

It's disconcerting when, for example, a board member leans forward on his elbows, looks the presenter of the budget straight in the eye with a little smirk on his face and says, "You mean to say that you don't know the cost of that item and you're in charge of the finances in that area".

Even if you are not easily angered, this approach will do it every time. The audacity! Most people presenting budgets will not have all of the detail available at their fingertips, especially in a very large organization. You might have a good estimate. The information is available from staff, but they probably would have left for the day. It was a good question. What is annoying is how and why it was asked. Are we naive in thinking that board members should be encouraging and supportive? Unfortunately, some are just the opposite.

Troublesome board members. They dominate the meetings. They tend to enjoy demeaning the staff. They are anything but supportive. So how does a board go about removing these ineffective and troublesome members?

Tenure

Perhaps the chairman should take them aside and suggest that they "shape up, or ship out". This is sometimes difficult, as the chairman may have even nominated the board member. In fact, some boards are so filled with friends that nobody wants to confront anybody on sensitive issues.

I have ruled out sending an anonymous note. The most realistic measure is tenure, setting a time limit on board membership. One board on which I served had no tenure provision. A founding director had been on the board since its inception over forty years ago! I have been on the board of the Canadian Council Of Christian Charities (CCCC) for over 15 years. That too is a long time to be on a board. If they had wanted to remove me, it could not have been accomplished without using provisions in the bylaws that relate to board members being insane, bankrupt, criminals, or dead. (Have you ever wondered why a board member who has died would want to stay on the board anyway?) I have not fallen into any of these categories yet. However, the CCCC has recently introduced tenure for board members, requiring each to resign for at least a year. Reappointment is possible. The forced resignation would take place after several years on the board (usually three to five years).

Tenure is something I did not support until recently. Two boards on which I served were working boards. The organizations were new and had few or no operating staff. When a board member left, it was like losing a staff member. Who would do the work? So we tended to keep our board members as long as possible. Tenure not only allows new members to join a board and bring fresh ideas, it also provides a way out of the dilemma of removing those ineffective and troublesome board members. Many organizations have now incorporated a tenure clause into their bylaws. At the same time, effective board members can always be placed on a committee while they are off the board.

WHOSE MEETING IS IT ANYWAY?

"Hi Alf. How are you doing"?

"Not too bad, Ken. How about you"?

"Business is good, but the bank sure is getting tight with its money".

"Ken. The reason I called is to let you know that we need to prepare the minutes of the annual meeting. For the record, you know".

"Sure Alf. Why don't you just go ahead and prepare them the same as last year"?

"What do you think would be a good date to show for the meeting"?

"Why not February 26. It isn't a holiday or a weekend".

"Sounds good to me. I'll go ahead and have the minutes typed and send them over to you for a signature. Send them back as soon as possible and I'll put them in the minute book".

That is the way we used to prepare the minutes of the annual meeting when I was operating my own business. The lawyer would send the typed minutes to me, they would be signed and returned to him and he would see that they were put into the official minute book. My partner and I were the only board members. The contents of the minutes were of little importance, as long as we did not have to deal with share transfers or other special items. In practical terms, whenever my partner and I discussed any business matters it was a directors' meeting. In a charitable organization the board meetings are more than that – they are meetings of the board, called by the board.

There are some CEOs who feel that they should arrange the board meetings, set the agenda and even decide what time to have coffee breaks. I like cooperation when it comes to arranging board meetings. That cooperation should be between the CEO and the board chairman. But, it is a board meeting for the board and should be arranged only under board direction. The bylaws of most organizations usually spell that out. I think it is quite appropriate for the CEO to give administrative support to the board chairman in arranging the meeting. But the chairman must have the final say when it comes to what items are placed on the agenda. Obviously, if there is a good relationship between the CEO and the board (especially the chairman) there will be no problem for the CEO to have his items placed on the agenda. But the final approval of any agenda has to rest with the chairman.

While I was chairman of the CCCC board, the CEO usually prepared the agenda of the board meetings and reviewed it with me. I appreciated the support given by the CCCC office, but we always understood that the final approval of any agenda belonged to the chairman. However, we should not ignore the fact that the CEO is probably the most informed person when it comes to operational items on the agenda on which he and his staff would report. We should also recognize that the chairman is going to be responsible for leading and controlling the meeting. For this reason alone, he needs to have some part in preparing the agenda.

During the meeting the board may want to sit "in camera", (only board members are in attendance). These are times when issues are sensitive enough to require that no staff members be present. Staff should never feel slighted if asked to leave a board meeting. I have never been in a board meeting where they have discussed my salary. I have also been asked to leave meetings when the board wanted to discuss disciplining another board member. As chairman of one board, I did not hesitate to ask staff to leave the meeting while we discussed their performance and reviewed their salary. Every board has the privilege of holding private discussions.

If the meeting belongs to the board, how can staff assist in making the meeting successful and meaningful from an administrative point of view? I believe that staff should perform as much of the preparatory work as possible. This can take many forms. For instance, sending out the materials in advance of the meeting should be handled by staff. Arranging for coffee breaks and lunch is another area of staff responsibility. Remember, board members are volunteers and many of them have other responsibilities related to business. Board activities have to be squeezed into very busy schedules.

WHERE SHOULD MEETINGS BE HELD?

The logical response to that question has to be, "Wherever we can have an effective and meaningful meeting at the least expense".

You cannot argue with that. However, this is not the only factor to be considered.

What about the meeting at a reasonably priced location where someone has to make a telephone call only to discover that the nearest telephone is at the service station ten miles down the road? Or maybe the washrooms are outdoors! This might be a wonderful retreat location, cheap and quiet, but it makes for a terrible meeting place. Sound extreme? Well, this is the way some boards think. Cost is the only factor as far as they are concerned. But what they save will soon be spent on a campaign to recruit new board members. Cost should be a factor, but not the only one.

My preference is to hold meetings in the organization's offices. There you have staff support throughout the day (and evening if required), telephones, stationery supplies, files for reference, etc. And the cost is minimal. One important thing to remember, however, is that staff have other responsibilities. When they are giving time to a board meeting their other work is being neglected. At World Vision, staff always gave willingly of their time to assist in preparing meetings held in the office. Of course there was the odd complaint of, "When do they expect me to get my regular work done"?

I often reminded my administrative assistant of the final point on her position description which stated, "And other duties as required". Also, you have to give staff time to prepare for these extra duties. Nobody appreciates being informed that lunch is being served to the board in half an hour and you need their help.

Of course, meetings are not always held during the day although it is much easier to obtain staff support at that time. The timing of the meetings must consider that some board members are unable to meet during the day because of business reasons.

Before World Vision had an office with a boardroom, meetings were held at a local hotel. The cost was minimal and the board only met three times a year. There are some advantages to meeting away from the office when the location is more accessible for board members who are from out of town. A reasonably priced hotel should be considered that offers needed amenities and good administrative support. Meals are also easily obtained.

On one occasion we held a management meeting at a fairly expensive hotel. Some criticism was levied by certain board members because of the location. It was considered to be a poor decision even though discounted prices had been arranged. People outside of the organization would not have known about the cost reduction. It could appear to some that the organization was being careless with its funds. A good lesson was learned through this experience. Appearance is important.

If an organization appears to be careless in spending its funds, even when the facts do not substantiate this, it really does not matter to a donor. A meeting, accompanied by a nice dinner at a prestigious location, may be viewed with criticism by outsiders even if the costs are underwritten. Some board members object to this type of venue, and would refuse to accept an invitation to meet at some private club or other location which is not fitting to the image of the organization. It is never in the best interest of a charity to present itself as being affluent.

Board members must be commended who are willing and able to have the board meet at their business offices. Many businessmen are able and willing to do this and very often make the arrangements at their own expense.

BOARD MEMBER EXPENSES

If you served on the board of a charitable organization, would you expect to be paid? Of course not. A volunteer does not get paid. In my experience, I have never met a board member who expected to be compensated in any way for what he was doing for the organization. That does not mean that board members may never receive any benefit from serving. But they do not serve in order to receive a benefit.

On the other hand, a board member should not be expected to personally pay for expenses he incurs by attending board meetings. If that were the case, it would be difficult to attract people to serve, especially if they had to travel any distance to attend the meetings. We should not expect a board member in Vancouver to pay to attend a meeting in Toronto.

The cost of board meetings should be part of the organization's budget. This eliminates the problem of having to continually discuss these costs with board members.

Some board members will want to pay their own expenses when attending meetings. They should be encouraged to do so but they should not be asked to do so. If they do pay these expenses, I see no reason why they should not be able to receive a receipt for tax purposes from the charity. If the meeting expenses are a part of the budget then the board member's payment can be viewed as a donation.

If the organization has projects overseas, opportunities may be afforded board members to visit them. The treatment of expenses for board member visits of this nature has caused real concerns for some charities. The board should establish a policy to clarify how the charity will treat this issue. The board may decide that the organization should budget these costs as orientation of new board members. How often board members travel overseas would depend on the availability of funds.

It may be difficult to convince some donors that the organization's funds (the donor's gifts) should be spent in this manner. Some large charities are better able to justify this type of expenditure, but I believe donors would not continue to support the organization if they felt that their gifts were utilized in this way. Most board members would not expect the organization to pay for them to travel overseas. The board needs to be very clear on this matter. No board member should expect to receive any particular benefit by serving on the board of a charitable organization. However, no charitable organization should expect board members to serve at their own expense.

DIRECTORS AND OFFICERS LIABILITY INSURANCE

In the good old days, one thing you never worried about when joining the board of a charitable organization, was the possibility of being sued. I thought about many things before saying "yes" to an invitation to join a board, but never about having to protect myself against legal action. It has only been in the past few years that this has become a concern.

This particular issue came into focus through one particular case where the President of a company in Ontario was sued along with his company after an employee fell on the icy stairs at the front of the company offices. Seeking restitution for injury, the employee filed action against everybody, including the President. The court decided that the President had the authority and the responsibility to see that the steps outside the building were cleared of ice and snow. The decision that directors and officers could now be held responsible, along with their organizations, caused a ripple of concern throughout the legal profession. A warning went out:

"If you are on the board of any organization, you may be held personally responsible for any actions of that organization. The best thing to do is to purchase insurance to protect the directors and officers against personal legal attacks".

As was expected, the matter of purchasing Directors and Officers Liability Insurance suddenly appeared on many board meeting agendas. Board members were also being reminded by their legal advisors of their normal responsibilities as trustees of a charity. The laws pertaining to a trustee's responsibility were clear and it was usually only required to show that as board members (trustees) they acted with due diligence in protecting the assets of the organization. Except for criminal acts, most board members were not concerned about their role on the board until this recent case became an issue. With this added concern, many charitable organizations sought to acquire protection for board members and officers.

Directors and Officers Liability Insurance is not easily obtained. There are very few insurance companies offering it. The application procedures are somewhat tedious, requiring the filing of several detailed forms. Board members may also be required to file individual statements with the application.

Like any insurance policy, there are many variations and endorsements available. However, there are several key points that every organization must consider related to this type of insurance.

The coverage is subject to exclusions, but generally the insurance company agrees to "pay all loss that the directors and officers shall become legally obligated to pay as a result of any claim or claims made against them for a wrongful act". A "wrongful act" is defined as: "The term WRONGFUL ACT means libel, slander or defamation of character, any breach of duty, neglect, error, misstatement, misleading statement, omission or other act done or wrongfully attempted by the Directors and Officers in the discharge of their duties solely in their capacity as Directors and Officers or any of the foregoing so alleged by any claimant or any other matter claimed against them solely by reason of their being such Directors or Officers". (It sounds like an insurance policy.)

One such policy goes on to state, "...to defend any suit instituted in Canada against the Directors and Officers seeking damages payable under the terms of this policy...and to reimburse the directors and officers for the costs, charges and expenses incurred in defending actions, suits or proceedings against the Directors and Officers before Criminal Courts if the defense of such actions, suits or proceedings proves to be fully successful".

And that is only a small portion of the text!

Similar to other insurance coverage, it is possible to purchase various limits of liability, and there are provisions for deductibles. The premiums would be based on the amount of coverage and the organization's income. For some of the larger charities the cost could amount to several thousand dollars a year.

On most policies several insurance companies share the risk. I am aware of one policy in which five insurance companies are each sharing twenty per cent of the risk.

Every organization has to determine its own course of action. What should your organization do? Can it afford the coverage? Can the board members and officers risk going without this protection? The question must be asked though, "would you purchase automobile insurance even if you have never had an accident, or house insurance, if you have never had a fire?" Every board must at least consider the options available to it. If a board decides that liability insurance is not necessary, it must ensure that every board member understands the risk they face by being on that board. The risk may not be great, but there is a risk and this risk is greater today than it was a few years ago.

The board should research the matter. Get advice from an insurance agent. Obtain some quotes. If the board is going to decide against coverage, they should at least make the decision after gathering all the facts. Until a very large claim is lodged against the board members or officers of a Canadian charity, this matter will not be given the degree of attention it deserves. It is possible, however, that some people may refuse to serve without this protection. When that first large claim is levied against a charity in Canada, every board will be reviewing its liability coverage and every board member will be considering his future as a board member.

This chapter has dealt with several important matters related to board membership, none of which should be considered lightly. If you are on a board, stop and consider how effective you are and how much you are contributing to the organization. I hope you will be motivated to review the board functions within your organization with the goal of improving the process.

3

Taking out the Garbage – A Board or Management Responsibility

"POLICY – A course of action, guiding principle, or procedure considered to be expedient, prudent or advantageous". (Houghton Dictionary)

It had started to snow around noon. The staff were becoming concerned about the predictions of more snow and heavy winds. Many of them had to drive to communities outside of the Mississauga area and wanted to get away from the office early. They were aware of the "early closing policy" and were waiting in anticipation of an announcement over the public address system. I liked this policy. It was only invoked during the winter months, and then only infrequently, but the decision to invoke it was mine.

Several of the staff would mention to me that weather conditions were getting worse and driving home would be very slow and dangerous, at the same time reminding me that I didn't have to worry because I lived around the corner from the office. I enjoyed the playful interaction knowing that in due time I would announce the office closure. With much fanfare I would proceed to the reception desk, take the microphone and announce, "Due to the very severe weather conditions and my compassion, the office is closing and all

staff are free to go". Relishing in the thanks from staff as they left
the office I remembered that I was just following policy.

While an organization's board sets policy for the organization, it is
management's responsibility to formulate operational guidelines.
There is a definite difference between policies and guidelines, but
defining that difference can be a problem. The drafting and clarifying
of policies can take months of board and staff time. But however
long it takes, it should be done. No organization can operate effectively without clearly defined policies and guidelines. The definition
of board policy and operational guideline may differ between organizations. Through my experience as a board member and manager, I
have followed several principles in developing board policies and
operational guidelines.

POLICIES

The board of directors determines the policies which guide the
CEO in overall operation of an organization.

Board policies apply to principles and fundamentals of the organization's purpose, scope and function and take precedence over operational guidelines.

Board policies impact upon several significant areas:
• Determination of the organization's purposes and goals.
• Budgeting, fund raising, fiscal accountability and investments.
• Relationships with constituents and other organizations.
• Qualifications and responsibilities of the CEO and other officers
of the organization.
• The public image of the organization.
• A monitoring of management's effectiveness.

GUIDELINES

Operational guidelines define actions and procedures by which management gives oversight to the day to day operation of the organization.

The CEO approves operational guidelines and ensures that there is
no conflict between the guidelines and the board policies.

Operational guidelines cover several significant areas:
• The organization's relationships with its constituents and other
organizations.

• Personnel matters including hiring and firing, compensation, training, benefits, etc.
• The corporate culture and relationships between staff.
• The accountability of management as governed by board policies that set operational standards.
Guidelines originate within the management group which is responsible for implementing them.

BOARD POLICIES

There is often difficulty in determining policies that are the responsibility of the board and guidelines that are operational or the responsibility of management. This grey area will always exist. Unfortunately, where there is doubt in this area, the board usually assumes responsibility, often at the expense of upsetting management. Separating policies from guidelines may be difficult, but I consider the following major areas to be board responsibilities.

(a) Fiscal Year End

Although the bylaws of the organization usually establish this, the board is responsible for determining the organization's year end. There are legal implications to be considered in determining this date, and any change in the date requires filing supplementary letters patent if the organization is incorporated.

(b) Audit Committee

Most organizations should have an audit, and in many instances an audit is required by law. The board (or the corporation members in some organizations) is responsible for appointing the auditors. An Audit Committee is something every organization should have, and appointing this committee is the board's responsibility. The committee is usually appointed annually and consists of not less than three members, two of whom would be from the board, one being the Treasurer. This allows for someone outside of the board to be a member.
The committee's mandate would include:
1. Reviewing the annual financial statements and auditor's report prior to recommending their approval to the board.
2. Establishing the terms of the audit engagement.

3. Reviewing the auditor's Management Letter and following up the recommendations.

4. Ensuring the adequacy of internal accounting controls.

The board should have a written mandate for this committee.

Membership on this committee should be restricted to those who have more than a passing interest in financial matters. I have had experiences in which committee chairmen had no background in finance and should never have been appointed. The appointment was based on a particular person's availability and willingness to serve. What was needed, however, were members who understood the financial statements and could ask pertinent questions.

The Treasurer should have a direct link to the auditors on matters such as the setting of the audit scope and any other special assignments that the board may want the auditors to perform. However, management is usually more directly involved in the timing of the year end audit and working with the auditors on preparing the audited financial statements. Although the Treasurer can assign specific projects to the auditors, this should never be done without the knowledge of the CEO or the Chief Financial Officer, unless of course management is suspected of impropriety.

The audited financial statements should be reviewed by the Treasurer in a meeting between management and the auditors, followed by a meeting of the Audit Committee. In this way, the Treasurer is presenting the financial statements to the Audit Committee. The Audit Committee then presents them to the board through the Treasurer. If everyone's responsibilities are set out properly, the year end audit should go smoothly. The establishment of an Audit Committee is one of the requirements for charities to obtain and retain usage of the CCCC Seal Of Financial Accountability.

(c) Conflict Of Interest

Although this is a board policy, it pertains to both board members and staff and usually states that they agree to place the welfare of the organization above personal interests, interests of family members or others who may be personally involved in substantial affairs affecting the organization's basic functions.

The board members and staff are requested to fully disclose the precise nature of their interest or involvement when participating in any transaction for the organization in which another party to the transaction includes: himself or herself, a member of the family (spouse, parents, brothers, sisters, children, immediate relatives), or an organization with which the board member or staff member or family members are affiliated.

It is usually requested that disclosure be made at the first knowledge of the transaction.

There is substantial detail that can go into formulating this type of policy. For instance, what constitutes being affiliated with an organization that is doing business with your organization? In some cases it has been determined that disclosure should be made if the board member or staff member is an officer, director, trustee, partner, employee or agent of such an organization, or is a consultant for such an organization.

When a conflict of interest does exist and is reported, how should it be handled? Practically, it could be handled by the CEO and reported to the board with the information being held in the strictest confidence.

If there is a possible conflict of interest, the party involved must refrain from participating in considering the proposed transaction, assuming that it is reported prior to the transaction taking place. Of course, they also would not participate in any vote to determine how to proceed with the matter.

Annually, each member of the board and management should complete a Disclosure Letter which indicates any possible areas of conflict. Possible conflicts of interest that arise during the year should be reported to the CEO or board chairman within 30 days of occurrence.

The penalty for not complying with this policy should be made quite severe. In some cases, not reporting such conflicts could result in removal from the board or having employment terminated.

Particular areas of possible conflict of interest, for instance, might involve board members offering legal, insurance or investment services. On any board you will probably find a lawyer, or an insurance agent or a banker, or someone who works in the investment field.

What is a conflict of interest? It usually means that the board or staff member or his family will derive some financial benefit from the organization by virtue of the fact he is associated with the organization. In some respects, being on the inside gives the board member certain financial advantages.

The Lawyer/Board Member

A few years ago the CCCC was attempting to determine whether a charity could be the trustee of its own trusts. There had never been a decision handed down by the courts establishing whether this could be done legally. It was decided that a test case was required. Who best to represent the CCCC in this matter than a lawyer who was on the board. But this created a dilemma.

The lawyer/board member would require a great deal of time to prepare the case. Would it be proper to ask him to do this free of charge? The board decided that this would not be appropriate. Conversely, if the lawyer/board member was paid to represent the CCCC, the obvious conflict of interest troubled us as a board. Should he benefit financially because of his board membership? It would not look proper. So, if he does the work, he doesn't get paid and if he doesn't perform the work, the CCCC would have to engage a lawyer who is not nearly as familiar with the problem.

This was resolved by having the board offer the case to the lawyer on the board, with the understanding he wouldn't be involved in the discussion. In fact, he left the meeting while the discussion was held. The board voted in favour of him doing the work thus ensuring the work would be performed by the best available person at a reasonable fee. At the same time, the board member had no part in the decision. A fact that was duly recorded in the board minutes.

The Insurance Agent/Board Member

Every organization has insurance needs. Who best knows that need than the insurance agent on your board? There are many organizations that obtain good insurance advice from board members, but these same members should not be involved in writing policies for the organization. When the CCCC was developing its group insurance and pension plans the board used an outside consultant even though it had resources available to it within the board.

The Investor/Board Member

The whole matter of investments has also created problems for organizations over the years, especially for those that have knowledgeable people on their boards who could supervise investments through companies that employed them. Charitable organizations need assistance when it comes to investments. It is a specialized field and making wrong decisions can be costly. In fact, the trust laws that govern charities could cause legal problems for the organization's management and board if unwise investments are made.

Who best to give advice on investments than a board member who works in that field? My suggestion is that he only gives advice. This can be done personally or through the Investment Committee that he probably chairs. But I do not agree with investing the organization's assets in a company with which he is associated.

In one case with which I am familiar the Treasurer of the board worked for a brokerage firm. The organization's excess funds were invested with this company. This allowed the Treasurer to give oversight to the management of the investments, and to monitor investment decisions. Not a bad idea. Except, what if some enquiring reporter discovers this relationship while doing an article on the charity? Can you see the headline? "TREASURER OF CHARITY CONTROLS ITS FUNDS IN HIS COMPANY".

Now nothing has really happened here except that the board has made a bad decision. Good intentions, but a bad decision. The benefits to the charity may be maximized. But it does not look good to the outside world. There is nothing sinister about any of this, not even any thought of personal gain. But, it is the potential of abuse (appearance of evil) that could cause problems for the organization.

It should be noted that in this case the Treasurer could not financially benefit from this arrangement. He was an employee of a very large company and his only motive was to assist the charity.

Is it proper for boards to be sensitive about these matters? I think so, but you can see the dilemma it creates. Sometimes board members can do the best work for the organization because of their knowledge and expertise. I sympathize with professionals serving on boards who sometimes lose the opportunity for business because of this involvement. This is one of the costs of board membership.

Some organizations have gone to great lengths to deal with these issues. They have a board policy which clarifies how to handle transactions that appear to place a board member or staff member in conflict. How much detail should be in this policy? If your organization does not have a policy, one should be written.

This is how one charity dealt with it in their by-laws:

"It shall be the duty of every director of the council who is in any way, whether directly or indirectly interested in a contract or arrangement or proposed contract or proposed arrangement with the council (directors, members, subscribers) to declare such interest. When there is a conflict of interest the director must refrain from voting in respect of the contract or arrangement or proposed contract or proposed arrangement".

(d) Investments

As we have already noted, safeguarding the organization's assets should be of prime importance to the board. For this reason, every organization should provide management with some policies regarding the investment of funds, whether they are invested for a short term or long term. Oversight should be exercised through an Investment Committee.

It is obvious that good stewardship requires that excess funds be invested. Most boards would agree that this should be done in the short term to provide the best return and liquidity. In the longer term, investments should be made with a view to obtaining attractive returns consistent with strong investment diversification and risk control. This can be done by setting guidelines for the types of investments and the maximum proportions of each. For example, equities, 25% to 60%; bonds, 25% to 60%; not more than 30% in money market securities. These parameters should be reviewed in light of the particular needs and circumstances of the organization. There are many variations on this theme. Good counsel should be sought in determining what is best for your organization.

(e) Automobiles

If the organization provides a vehicle for the CEO or other staff, the board should establish policy guidelines. At one time a company car provided a substantial tax benefit to the employee. Revenue Canada has since managed to take away most of the advantage. I still think it is a good idea for an organization to offer a car to certain employees and in many cases automobiles are provided for the CEO and senior management as part of their compensation. Although there is now insignificant tax advantages for the employee, it is a major capital outlay that the employee does not have to face. With the price of cars today, I think this is a real benefit.

Board policy should make it clear what category of employee is eligible for this benefit. Some organizations stipulate the value (cost or lease) that will be allowed. Because the price of cars is changing frequently, a good approach is to stipulate the type of vehicle allowed and let management govern the actual procedures for providing the vehicles through its operational guidelines.

If the board has agreed to provide vehicles for certain staff, it is not necessary that they be involved in setting the guidelines by which this will be done. The board approves the budget for expenses in this area and this enables them to monitor this benefit.

(f) Human Resources

It is proper for the board to be involved in setting certain policy guidelines with respect to staff. The philosophy under which the organization functions in dealing with staff should be defined, and might include the following:

"The organization will provide salary and benefits at a level necessary to allow staff to devote their entire vocational lives and talents to the work of the organization. The organization strives to be fair and equitable in every respect in the treatment of its employees. Individual salaries will be based on evaluated positions and performance.

"The organization will provide salaries and benefits comparable to other similar organizations.

"Equal opportunity for training, advancement and remuneration will be practised".

The key here is that the board has given management some guidelines under which to operate. The board should not get involved with actual human resource functions. This is left to management.

(g) Mailing List

Most, if not all charitable organizations have a mailing list. It is the organization's channel through which it communicates with its supporters. Because of the sensitivity with which most donors treat the giving of their name to any organization, I think charities should promise the donor that it will not give his name to any other organization without permission. In this regard, the board policy might be developed to read, "The names and addresses of the donors shall be held in confidence and will not be revealed or exchanged with any other organization".

(h) Travel

In many organizations travel costs can be substantial. For this reason the board should outline some policy guidelines for management. Some suggestions:

Air Travel: Discounted fares should be obtained wherever possible. Normal class of travel will be economy.

Board Travel: Directors are encouraged to travel overseas to observe the organization's projects at least once in five years. Any board travel must be approved in advance by the board. (There may be some sensitivity in this area of board travelling at the expense of the organization. There are obvious advantages to both the board member and the organization, but these should be clearly defined for each trip. It should be recognized here as well that many board members would personally pay for such travel.)

Spousal Travel: In some organizations the board recognizes that there are certain circumstances where a spouse should accompany staff members who travel extensively as part of their job assignment. Not only is this good for a marriage, but in many instances the spouse can contribute to the organization by writing articles about the trip. Provision can be made to allow the CEO's spouse to travel with him, subject to board approval. Another approach might be to allow for one trip per year, with any additional requests to be considered by the board.

Other staff who travel extensively might be given this same opportunity. This can be monitored and approved by the CEO. A report of all international travel is made to the board by management on a regular basis.

These are just some of the possible areas for development of board policy. If your organization does not have properly defined board policies, you most likely will have the board involved in day-to-day operations. Clearly defined board policies are necessary to define the board's boundaries within the corporate structure.

Conversely, it is important that management develops operational guidelines to ensure that both the board and management are aware of staff responsibilities. Let's look at some of these guidelines.

OPERATIONAL GUIDELINES

(a) Audit and Legal Services

In many organizations it is necessary to clarify the responsibility for contacting the auditors and legal counsel. The cost alone of these professional services is reason enough to control their use. It is normally the responsibility of the Chief Financial Officer to have ongoing contact with the auditors. Engaging legal counsel may be left with the CEO depending on the organization's size. If the organization is large, the Chief Financial Officer would also have this responsibility.

Guidelines should recognize the privilege of the Treasurer, who is a board member, to have access to the auditors as required.

(b) Staff Training

There is no question as to the value of ongoing staff training. Organizations should encourage this activity and provide whatever support they can to assist staff members in increasing their skills, which will, in turn, increase their value to the organization. Enrolling in an accredited accounting course (such as CGA) would be an example of the type of continuing education that would benefit the employee and the organization. There may be occasions when the organization will ask a staff member to attend training sessions at the organization's expense. In larger organizations, in-house training may be available. My experience with this approach has been that it is not as successful and is often more costly than buying the expertise outside the organization.

Assistance to staff could be handled in several ways, including:

• At the beginning of the course, the organization will reimburse the employee 50% of the cost of the course and text books.

• Upon the successful completion of the course within the allowed time, the organization will reimburse the employee the remaining 50% of costs.

• Failure to complete the program, unless for justifiable reasons, will result in a request for a refund of any monies advanced.

Certain criteria should be met before a staff member can apply for this assistance, such as:

• The employee must be full-time, have been employed for at least six months and have completed their probationary period.

• The course must be recommended by the employee's manager and approved by management and/or Personnel Director.

• Requests for reimbursement of course costs are to be made in writing to the Personnel Department with supporting documentation, outlining the prescribed course of study, duration, costs, and benefits to the organization and to the employee.

(c) Dress

This is always a topic of interest within an office.

Most employees know how to dress properly in an office environment. However, there have been occasions when some staff members desire to be different or just don't care how they look. Mary was such a person.

Mary was somewhat stout, (to say the least). Because of her weight and size, bright yellow was not her colour. Several years ago, hot pants were the style for many young girls. Mary, however, was in her 30s. Well, you can guess what happened that unforgettable morning. Into the office walked Mary in a bright yellow hot pant outfit! It certainly gave the staff much to talk about that day and for several days after the event. To the other staff she became known as "Mary The Canary". Mary probably never realized the stir she caused within the office.

Organizations should not have to tell staff how to dress. Common sense should dictate this. But unfortunately, some staff do not use common sense. I have seen a white painter pants outfit on a clerk, complete with a strap on the side on which to hang a hammer! Shorts and bare feet are for the beach, but I have seen them in the office more than once.

All of these situations draw attention to the employee. If clothing does this, then I suggest it is not proper office attire.

In some offices men are required to wear ties. I know of one office where men are not allowed to be outside of their own work area without a jacket on. This is somewhat Victorian. Most men would willingly wear a shirt and tie (even though we have never been able to decide the purpose of a tie). There may be some jobs where this might not be practical, such as for an artist. Wearing blue jeans would not be on my recommended list of proper clothing for men (or women), unless the staff work in the warehouse or on maintenance. Because of the sensitivity of this matter a brief guideline should suffice.

"Employees are to dress with good taste and modesty.

"Dress restrictions are enforced in places where accidents or serious injury may occur".

Once a guideline has been developed, it should be conveyed to all staff. New staff should be told about the guideline during their initial orientation. The responsibility of monitoring this particular matter should be in the hands of the Personnel Department, but preferably the manager should handle situations as they occur.

(d) Employee Health and Safety

It is interesting to note that many organizations give little or no thought to this issue. Every organization should strive to provide the safest possible conditions within its office to meet legal requirements and to protect its staff. In doing so, a guideline should be written to explain how the organization is meeting this need. Such a guideline should include the following:

• "The organization will provide any training necessary to ensure each employee is thoroughly instructed in the operation of equipment, fire drill evacuation procedures and first aid procedures".

• "The organization requires that all injuries in the workplace be reported through the proper channels and followed up by management to ensure that the situation has been remedied, and if further action is necessary to improve safety, that this is taken in a timely manner".

• "The organization will provide an emergency first aid facility within the office".

• "The organization will provide first aid training to at least three staff members. A schedule indicating which person is responsible each month will be posted on the first aid room door and staff will be notified by memo".

This is a very important issue. If your organization has been lax in addressing the need for first aid within the office you will need only one bad experience to know that you are unprepared.

(e) Hiring Of Family Members

During my 15 years with World Vision all members of my immediate family, at one time or another, worked for the organization. I see nothing wrong with this. Of course, there is always the fear of nepotism (favouritism to relatives), but I have not seen this during my years in business. I think there is a definite benefit to having families involved in the same organization. In fact, IBM recognizes the value of having children follow in their parent's footsteps and give official recognition to these situations.

Most organizations would not prevent family members from working together. However, in such a situation guidelines should be established to ensure that the privilege is not abused. One way to present the matter could be:

"Family members of employees will be eligible for employment under the following guidelines:

• "Applications for employment will be processed under the same guidelines that exist for non-family members, without prejudice.

• "Family members will preferably be employed in different departments.

• "The hiring of family members is subject to the approval of management (or some other responsibility level)".

(f) Company Cars

We have already considered a board policy which set out guidelines on this matter. Now we will look at guidelines management could develop in keeping with board policy. Principles they might consider could include:

• The type of car selected by the staff member should be approved by management (usually the CEO or a vice-president). The CEO's car is approved by the chairman of the board.

• All vehicles would be purchased or leased bearing in mind the organization's image. Luxury cars would not be appropriate.

• All vehicles would be approved with certain equipment such as:
   ▪ automatic transmission
   ▪ power brakes
   ▪ power steering
   ▪ air conditioning
   ▪ AM/FM radio cassette
   ▪ side view mirrors

• The costs for additional equipment will be the responsibility of the employee and payment for such will be made at the time of acquisition.

• The standard term of lease will be 36 months.

• Business operating costs will be the responsibility of the organization.

• The organization will be reimbursed for personal use of the vehicle at a rate approved by the CEO. (This can easily be handled through payroll deduction.)

• Use of the vehicle is subject to restrictions imposed by the leasing company and insurance carrier.

• Accidents shall be reported promptly to the organization.

These guidelines have proven to be sufficient in most organizations. In some cases staff members are allowed to carry a company credit card to purchase gas. The employee then would pay for personal use of the car at a monthly rate established by the organization. Of course, when the employee is on vacation the credit card is not used.

There is a tendency to require extensive reporting by both the employee and organization. Reporting requirements should be kept to a minimum as long as government regulations are being met.

Also, the employee will be charged with a taxable benefit which must be included in calculating his earnings for tax purposes. This amount should be used in calculating the employee's tax deductions for each pay period. Operating costs as well as the standby charge are considered taxable benefits. Information can be obtained from Revenue Canada on this issue.

(g) Personal Sales

Have you ever been approached by another staff member about buying chocolate bars to support their child's school orchestra trip? This is not what we are referring to here. There is a problem however, if one of the staff members wants to sell Tupperware or Avon products in the office, especially on company time. I have had requests from staff for permission to set up displays in the lunch room to sell products. Although I do not have anything against free enterprise, it does create some problems. The major difficulty is saying "no" to the next request, once you have said "yes" to one. Also, there may be some products the organization would not want sold within the office. So a guideline was established during my time at World Vision:

• Sales of products could take place within the office for selected items.

• On-site sales of items which reflect a personal or organizational profit motive are not permitted. Such items would include those sold through mail order catalogues and pamphlets, for example.

• All sales activities must be approved by management prior to advertising them on the staff bulletin board. (In larger organizations the Personnel Department would give this approval.)

With any guideline, there must be flexibility. Each case should be decided on its own merit. But without some guideline, anything goes. These are just some of the operational guidelines that might be considered by any organization. Many more could be developed, depending on circumstances and need. The key issue here is that every organization should have written guidelines to assist management in making decisions in certain areas. Written guidelines will also help to avoid staff confusion on many matters.

CONCLUSION

Establishing areas of responsibility for the board and management is critical to every organization. Most conflicts and tensions between these two bodies can be attributed to the failure of having agreement on who is responsible for what.

Written policies and guidelines contained in a 'Policy Manual' and updated periodically, will assure that your organization reaches its objectives in a business-like manner.

4
Finding Staff That Make You Look Good

"PEOPLE ARE OUR MOST IMPORTANT PRODUCT"!

That is the slogan of a large steel company near Toronto. It's a good slogan. I respect the company, and I'm not a prospective buyer of their products. It makes me feel good because I also like people.

Years ago, there was a radio program hosted by Art Linklater, called People Are Funny. It featured the strange and funny things people do and was meant to make you laugh at people. People still do strange and funny things and some of them are probably working in your organization.

When I say people are funny, I mean that people are different from each other in the way they act, in what they say, and how they say it. They are also different in how they treat each other, what they expect from life, and what they expect from an employer.

As we delve into the realm of personnel issues, we must keep in mind that they affect staff, and staff are men and women, children, mothers and fathers, the young, the old and the handicapped.

Employees are real people – real flesh and blood people, part of God's creation. We must never lose sight of this fact.

Even though personnel matters are by their very nature business matters, no organization should ever forget that it is dealing with the lives of people in one way or another.

First Steps

An organization's need for staff becomes evident when there's work to be done and not enough people to do it. So, we pick up the phone, speak to a few of our friends, and tell them we need help. We might place an advertisement in a few magazines or newspapers.

So far, so good.

Then, the first call comes. "I read your ad for clerical help. What kind of work is it?"

"Well, we need someone to answer the phones. Oh, and we have a lot of filing that's piled up. And then there's getting the mail ready to go out each day...and then..."

Hold it! Do you know what you're doing here? You're describing a job. If you had written all that down you would have what is known as a Position Description.

Unfortunately, too many organizations can describe the position over the phone but have never documented the job responsibilities. I know many employees in different organizations that do not have a written Position Description. They know what they are supposed to do, but none of it is documented. This leads to countless difficulties for both the organization and the employee. So, even before that ad is placed, or that phone call is made to friends, we need to prepare a position description.

POSITION DESCRIPTIONS

"How many of your staff have position descriptions?", I asked the manager.

"I think three out of the five staff, but I don't have one. I've discussed the need with my boss for over two years, but we haven't had time to prepare it".

When I asked another staff member the same question, she responded:

"They told me during the interview what they wanted me to do, but I have never had anything in writing. Oh, except in my employment letter it does state the title of my position".

I asked several managers and staff of a large organization if they thought that everyone should have a position description and they all agreed that they should. I asked them why. Most of the responses were related to the need for an employee to know what is expected of them in their job. None of them gave any thought to what other purposes a position description could serve.

Besides letting an employee know exactly what responsibilities the job carries, a position description can be used for setting salary levels within the organization. In addition, it identifies who the person reports to, what the qualifications are for the position, and what interaction the person has with other people, both inside and outside the organization.

There are several methods available by which you can evaluate positions, but unless you have position descriptions in place, it is nearly impossible.

An employee cannot be properly evaluated if there is no position description against which their performance can be measured. The factors used in evaluating the position include education, job complexity, the contribution of the job to the organization, contacts with others, the environment in which the job takes place, and the number of people reporting to the position. All of these factors are taken into account, valued, and the position is scored. The number of points it receives places it in a grade scale for determining salary.

A position description describes the job responsibilities, not how the job is performed. A well-written position description will contain no more than ten points. Procedures are another matter. Do not mix them with the description of the position responsibilities.

Staff members should be involved in writing their own position description. It is sometimes very enlightening to see what staff are doing as opposed to what management thought they were doing. A staff member will more readily accept a position description to which they have contributed. This also provides an opportunity to discuss differences in perceptions of the job that might exist between management and staff.

Every employee should have a copy of their position description. The content of the position description should be reviewed at least annually to ensure that the responsibilities have not changed. If they have changed, it could alter the value of that position, resulting in the employee being underpaid (or overpaid) at that particular time.

I'm a stickler for position descriptions. In every job I've held I've had a position description, except when I owned my own company.

I never forced myself to prepare one, but I also made sure I wasn't underpaid!

New pay equity legislation in certain provinces of Canada requires organizations to have position descriptions for all jobs. If your organization does not have a position description for every job, including the CEO, it should be a priority to prepare them.

SALARY GRADE LEVELS

Now that we have a position description for all positions within the organization, how do we go about setting proper salary grade levels? Note, I did not say 'salaries', I said 'salary levels'. There is a difference.

What Are Others Doing?

A good place to start is to see what other organizations are doing. For example, where do we go to see what the salary levels are for secretaries? Check some surveys. These can be obtained from the Board of Trade and consulting companies. Look specifically at your geographic area as there are regional salary differences.

You could also call a few of your friends in other organizations to see what they pay. Unless they are really good friends, however, they may not be so willing to share this information with you. Religious organizations, in particular, seem to have a fear of others knowing what their salary levels are. I've come to the conclusion that many of them are probably embarrassed because they pay so poorly or don't know why they pay at the levels they do. Not long ago, the Canadian Council of Christian Charities asked a room full of executives how many would like to participate in a salary survey. About eight hands were raised. The survey never took place.

Larger organizations such as World Vision are frequently contacted by other agencies asking advice on salaries and salary levels. They have never hesitated to share this information in confidence. But, if you are looking to other organizations to assist you in this area, you may find that only a few are willing to cooperate.

Setting Salary Levels

Salary levels should be established to include the lowest paying job and the highest paying job. For instance, if a secretary in Level 1 is promoted to President, she would perhaps move up to Level 15.

Each level should have a minimum, median and maximum value. This allows for employees to be placed somewhere within their level based on factors such as education and performance, so that two people in the same salary level can be paid different salaries determined by these various factors. The dollar differences between the minimum, median and maximum levels in each grade need to be established. One method of accomplishing this is to use a fifteen percent differential between each figure. For example, if in one grade level the minimum was $10,000, the median would be $11,500 and the maximum $13,225.

The difference between grade levels could be set at an eight percent variance. If the Level 1 minimum was $10,000, the Level 2 minimum would be $10,800. There are different ways to calculate these ranges and advice should be sought from professionals who work in salary administration.

Let's assume that we have established a position description for the secretary job. It is graded at Level 5 which has a minimum salary level of $20,000, the median is $23,000 and the maximum is $26,450 (using the fifteen percent factor). When applicants for the position ask about the salary, you can say it is in the $20,000 to $23,000 range, depending on experience, etc.

This may all sound very fundamental, but it is surprising that many organizations, especially non-profits, do not have position descriptions or have any idea of how to evaluate a position. A quick call to a friend asking "how much do you pay your secretary?", may be the extent of the research. I think this is quite inadequate and not entirely fair to the prospective employee.

Evaluation Factors

In other areas of the world other factors are often taken into consideration in establishing salaries. While consulting with a large organization in Europe, I discovered that individual salaries are often determined using factors such as age, marital status, size of family, and even whether a spouse is employed or not. These may be reasons to determine salary in Europe, but they would not be acceptable in North America.

For example, take two people performing similar jobs, having the same expertise and equally productive. One is a man with a family of five, the other a single woman. In Europe the man would probably be paid a higher salary than the woman. Is this equitable? I don't think so.

If one of your employees came into your office and asked for an increase in salary on the basis that he needed a new car, should he get an increase? I have never been able to justify a salary level on the financial needs of an employee. Doing so would lead to all kinds of problems. The only equitable approach is to value the position and pay according to the contribution that the employee brings to that position.

Shortly after receiving my CA designation, I was employed by one of my former clients, a small business with several office staff for whom I was responsible. One of these staff members entered my office one day and timidly stated, "My wife told me I should ask for a raise today". I don't remember the exact discussion that followed except this fellow did not remain with the company very long after this event.

I did learn early in my management career that there has to be a better reason for giving salary increases than "my wife told me to ask". For 25 years since that event I have never had a similar request, and if I had, it would still not have resulted in a salary adjustment.

Freezing Salaries

There may also be occasions when an individuals' salary should be frozen. This happens infrequently, but may occur when the employee has been with the organization for many years and has, because of length of service, reached the maximum salary level or even exceeded it. The problem becomes more evident when others are receiving annual cost of living increases and this particular employee receives nothing. The best thing you can do for these employees is to encourage them to increase their skills so they become promotable.

RECRUITING

Now that we have position descriptions and salary grades that classify the positions in the organization, we can go ahead and recruit.

Use Of Professionals

Depending on the size of an organization, recruiting may be carried out in many different ways. The larger, more affluent organizations might be able to afford professional recruiters, but charities seldom use them because of the cost. There may be specialized jobs where it might be extremely difficult to find qualified staff such as data processing specialists with particular skills. In cases like this, organizations have had to turn to professional recruiters for assistance. But in most cases, staff needs are met through other recruitment methods.

A few years ago the board of World Vision faced a most difficult challenge – replacing its CEO. Several steps were taken to initiate this process. A letter was circulated throughout Canada to many friends of the organization asking for the names of possible candidates. A professional recruiter was hired. It took over a year for the board to finally make a decision. Perhaps they had set their sights to high, determining that someone could be found with every qualification they required. This was an impossible goal.

During the process the recruiter became somewhat disenchanted with the indecisiveness of the board. Several candidates he presented were turned down. Even I was interviewed. I was disappointed with the process. There seemed to be an insensitivity to senior staff, as very little was conveyed to them about what was taking place. Several of us felt that a decision could have been made much sooner than it was. One of the vice-presidents was finally appointed and it was a good decision.

I believe in hiring from within an organization if suitable candidates are available. Many staff could not understand why the board did not see the value in this at the beginning of the process. We had a man who had many years of experience in overseas work and had proven himself in leadership. The unfortunate result of this delayed decision, was to give the newly appointed CEO the feeling that he was not the board's first choice and had been appointed only because nobody else was available. To make matters worse, there were indications that the board was not unanimous in its decision. This is not a good way for a new CEO to commence a relationship with his board.

Networking

One effective method of recruiting is to utilize your network of contacts, which could include other organizations and even present staff. Spread the word among as many as possible. Many top notch employees have been acquired through networking.

Advertising And Human Rights Issues

Paid advertising in periodicals and newspapers is another option.

Although I speak from my experience in the religious sector, many organizations are governed by a particular religion or creed which is necessarily part of its ethos and cannot be separated from its activities.

How can an organization structure an advertisement in the secular press to attract only those people who share the same beliefs as the organization? For instance, some magazines and newspapers will not allow the use of the term "Christian" because it is perceived to be in contravention of Human Rights legislation. Publishers have some freedom in how they interpret this, but many of them would not accept an advertisement that included the word "Christian".

Several years ago World Vision was advertising for a Controller and we wanted a Chartered Accountant. The best place to find a CA would be through an ad in the CA magazine. Responses would obviously be received from non-Christians, but I thought I could eliminate some of that problem by wording the advertisement in such a way as to encourage responses mainly from Christians. I submitted the advertisement to the magazine using the words, "A Christian organization", which legally, it is. In fact, the word "Christian" is in the incorporating documents.

The magazine called me to explain that they were unable to run the advertisement worded the way it was. They objected to the word "Christian". I argued on the grounds of our legal charter, but the magazine did have the right to decide what advertising was acceptable and it had decided that ours was objectionable. I felt I had a good case and contemplated seeking legal advice. This was discrimination! However, there must be a better solution. So I arranged a compromise with the magazine. We changed the word "Christian" to "religious". This was acceptable to the magazine, as now anyone who thought themselves religious could apply. I was expecting that the name of the organization would be recognizable by most of those who read the ad and that they would know it was a Christian organization.

Several responses were received and a qualified Christian was hired.

A great deal could be said about human rights issues facing organizations today but it is important to remember that many organizations do have the right to discriminate in their hiring practices.

Organizations should be discreet in their hiring practices so as not to bring attention to this issue. There will always be applicants for positions that will have views contrary to the organization.

How these situations are handled will determine whether a rejected applicant will contact the Human Rights Commission or not.

Visits From The Human Rights Commission

I sent an application to one respondent from my CA advertisement. Instead of completing it and returning it to me, he forwarded it to the Human Rights Commission with a formal complaint because the application asked questions about his religious beliefs. The gentleman was upset.

This all came to light when I received a call from the Human Rights Commission saying that one of their investigators was coming to see us. In fact, two came to meet with me. After a two hour discussion in which I defended our right to hire Christians, the one investigator in charge leaned over to me and quietly said, "I know the problem". It was obvious that this was not the first time the Commission had dealt with cases like this. We never heard any more about that particular complaint because the complainant had never completed the application form and returned it to us, and therefore had never been officially rejected. However, we were advised by the Commission that perhaps we should separate the religious questions from the official employment application form, which we did, although our legal counsel advised that this was not necessary.

A similar situation arose during the Ethiopian famine in late 1984. Many Canadians were anxious to assist, both financially and by offering to go to Ethiopia personally. A man applied for a position with World Vision in Ethiopia. Although he had good qualifications, someone else was offered the position who was not only better qualified but an Ethiopian. A problem arose when the unsuccessful candidate complained to the Human Rights Commission that he had been denied employment on religious grounds. The complaint was investigated by the Commission.

Although at one point in the investigation it was suggested that a cash settlement to the individual might allow the commission to close its file, we decided to stand our ground. Two factors were put forward in our argument: 1. World Vision is a Christian organization, and as such, had the right to discriminate, and, 2. all employment contracts for overseas jobs were handled by the international office in the United States, and they would ultimately determine who was hired. The Canadian office was not hiring, only screening candidates.

For the past six years, there has been a lot of correspondence flowing between the commission and the organization's lawyers. The case has never been taken to a formal hearing, although the Commission had suggested this would be a next step. The organization replied that if a formal hearing was held, it would file a counter suit for cost. The complaint was obviously an attack against Christianity, not the organization.

Over the years Commission staff have visited World Vision just to see what makes the organization tick. The visit is usually due to a change in Commission staff. They offer advice on discrimination and then leave the organization alone for another year or two.

This is a sensitive issue and one with which organizations should be familiar, especially those working from a particular religious ethos. A lawyer should be consulted in dealing with any human rights issue.

INTERVIEWING

An important part of recruiting is the interview process.

Who Interviews?

The person to whom a potential employee reports must be involved in the interview process. In my experience, the best candidates have been hired when more than one person is involved in the interview. This can be done by both interviewers at the same time, although it also can be carried out individually. Again, much depends on the size of the organization. If it is large enough to have a Personnel Department, the process is fairly defined. The Personnel Department would perform the initial screening and present only suitable candidates to the manager of the hiring department. In smaller organizations, the CEO might have to do all of the hiring. But even in that situation, if the person being hired is going to work for someone other than the CEO, that manager must be part of the process.

Check References

Often references are not contacted, or if they are, it is not done thoroughly. If you ask for references, take the time to contact them, or at least some of them. This should be standard practice. I have been used as a reference many times. Recently, one of my former staff members advised me that my name had been given as a reference for a position she was seeking. To my surprise, I received a call from the prospective employer, which in itself was not unexpected. But I was working in Europe at the time. This company, knowing the importance of following up references, tracked me down overseas. I was impressed with their diligence.

Testing

If your organization is not performing skill testing on applicants, now would be a good time to start. There are a number of simple tests available on the market. The results of these tests very often make the difference as to whether candidates are hired or not. Of course, if you have only one candidate and a heavy workload, you may not care too much how the candidate scores in the tests. Only the person responsible for hiring can make a decision as to whether to wait for a better candidate or hire the best person available at the present time.

The Employment Letter

Once the candidate has been chosen, he should be contacted by telephone. This should be followed by an employment letter confirming his hiring. This procedure is optional in the case of junior positions. However, many organizations send letters to every new employee. This provides an opportunity to verify discussions that have taken place and other important matters such as salary, vacation allowance and other benefits. Included in this letter is a reference to the probation period. (Every organization should have a probation period during which new staff are assessed.) Under Canadian labour law, it is much easier to terminate an employee during their probation period, than after it is completed. In most cases, this period would be three months. Many organizations extend this probation period to six months for senior positions.

Unsuccessful candidates can also be notified by letter, although there are many organizations that prefer to contact each candidate by telephone to advise them of the results of the interview. Under no circumstances should unsuccessful candidates be left without being advised.

The offer letter should be also be signed by the new employee indicating their agreement with the terms of employment and then it should be placed in their personnel file. This may seem like an unnecessary procedure, but many organizations have been able to refer to these letters to resolve future conflicts between staff and employer.

Delays Can Be Costly

A note of caution. Do not let the recruitment interview process take too long. Many good candidates have been lost to an organization because they found another job while waiting to hear about their interview. Also, do not make unrealistic promises about contacting a candidate within a few days when you know the process will take two weeks. The credibility of some organizations has been damaged because of their treatment of candidates.

The organization now has a new staff member with a proper position description who has been evaluated and placed in a salary grade level. The employee knows the salary range of the position, what grade level it is in, and who he reports to. There is no question about the probation period or the benefits because they were clearly outlined in the letter from the employer. Now it is time to go to work.

The challenge we now face is how to retain the person we have just hired.

5
Keeping Staff Even When They Don't Want to Stay

ORIENTATION

Month end was always a busy time for us in the catering business. We had financial statements to prepare for our clients, so the accounting staff usually had to put in extra hours during the first week of the month. Joan, our new receptionist/secretary, had stayed late to assist in the many calculations that were required. When I walked out of my office I had to pass her desk. What a mess! She had adding machine tape all over her desk, flowing onto the floor. Having been encouraged by the accounting staff, I asked her, "In your orientation did anyone tell you about our adding machine tape policy?"

"Not really", she responded as she looked up from her work.

"Well, during this period of tight money... you know the economy is not so good, so we really need to keep costs to a minimum. This month we are rolling up all of the adding machine tape so we can use the other side".

As her chin dropped and the colour of her complexion began to redden, I heard her say, "You must be kidding". I made a hasty exit back to my office.

It took only two minutes. There she was standing in front of my desk with an adding machine tape partially rolled up. "If you think I'm going to stay here all night and roll up paper, you better find yourself another secretary! If I had been told about this policy during my orientation, I would never have taken the job", she said.

When she heard the laughter from the accounting staff standing at the door she realized it was a joke, although it did take her a couple of days to see the humour in it herself.

The point is, it is important that new employees know all that they need to know about the organization and its policies as soon as possible after their first day on the job.

For some organizations, giving a new employee orientation means telling them where the coffee pot and the washrooms are located. And for some staff, that's all they really want to know. But there has to be more to it than that. The information given in the employment letter is not all that inclusive. It gives details on the major points regarding the organization's benefits, but little more. So when a new employee starts at the office on that first day, what do we do with them?

In a small office there is no problem introducing them to the other staff. The CEO can walk into the office with the new employee and say, "Hello, Mary. This is Susan. She will be working with you. Show her what to do. Hope you two get along". That's it. Mary tells Susan everything there is to know about the organization and the work.

In a larger organization, someone from the Personnel Department brings the new staff member to the manager after a basic form of orientation. The manager introduces the new staff member to the other staff in the department, who will soon teach him more about the organization and the work.

Starting to work for a small or a large organization doesn't appear to be that different, does it? It really isn't. But it should be. Orientation is not just introducing new staff to present staff and hoping they will learn about the organization from the "old-timers". Some form of orientation should be arranged for all new employees which would describe the work of the organization, its ethos, its policies, and so on. This cannot be accomplished through a simple introduction to co-workers on starting day.

The bad habits of the present staff, if there are any, along with the complaints and misconceptions about the organization, are usually passed on to new staff members quickly. Management should have a plan whereby all pertinent information about the organization is conveyed to new staff early on in their employment.

During the first few days, the organizational structure should be explained. It is always good to know who the CEO is, in case you meet him in the hall. A review of the organizational chart will explain the authority structure of the organization...(who's in charge of what).

The new employee should also become familiar with the organization's major policies, especially those affecting staff. Hopefully, these documents are in a manual, but this is not usually the case. Many organizations have policies but they fail to document them formally, and usually fail to tell new employees what they are. The new employee only finds out when he contravenes one of them.

The various things that are important to new staff would include:
• how staff are evaluated and how often
• punctuality
• sick leave and absenteeism
• coffee breaks
• acceptable dress
• personal use of photocopier
• personal phone calls
• parking
• lunch hour

This is only a partial list but new employees should not have to find out about these things through trial and error or discussions with co-workers.

I have given orientation to groups of 20 or more employees at a time. They did not all start on the same day, but it would be impossible for senior management to give orientation every time someone new started. The logical approach in larger organizations is to have the critical matters covered by the Personnel Department during that first couple of days, then a more extensive orientation is conducted a few weeks later.

Orientation with the CEO is mandatory. There is no better way to instill into the minds of new employees the ethos of the organization, than to have them spend some time with the leader of that organization. CEOs must find the time to do this.

Using videos is another way for the new staff to learn about the organization's activities.

If your organization does not have a formal orientation program of some kind, it should start one. I would commence by documenting all of those things that a new staff member should be made aware of during that most important first week of employment. This critical first week could make the difference as to whether or not a new employee remains with the organization for any meaningful length of time.

BENEFITS

Usually people do not decide to go to work for an organization simply because of the benefits. However, many organizations take advantage of their staff by not giving them what might be considered reasonable benefits. I am speaking here of various types of perks, including those required by government regulations. Of course, the government requires employers to pay Unemployment Insurance and Canada Pension Plan premiums and mandatory provincial health benefit premiums in some provinces. What else can an organization do for its employees? With many organizations, it is a matter of cost. Following are some options.

Group Insurance

Organizations can offer their employees some type of group insurance plan. These plans offer life insurance, accidental death and dismemberment insurance, dependent life insurance, long term disability protection, extended health care and dental care. Usually, if the organization is providing this coverage for its employees, the employee has the option of participating. There are very few organizations today that do not offer their employees at least this type of protection. One major factor regarding group insurance plans is how much of the cost the employee is asked to contribute. This is something that only the organization can determine, based on what it can afford. An insurance agent can discuss the various available options and the costs involved.

The CCCC offers a good plan. Several years ago the board met with representatives of a large insurance consulting company to discuss the idea of initiating a group plan for its member organizations. Since its inception, the plan has been considerably enhanced. One of the advantages of this type of large group plan is the lower costs and broader benefits, due to the larger number participating. Costs can be minimized and the plan written in such a way as to offer various options from which each organization can choose. The options under the CCCC plan have been expanded to include vision care and coverage for overseas workers. Each organization can choose its own options and the cost to the organization depends on how much they require their employees to contribute.

Pension Plans

A pension plan is another way of providing a major benefit to employees. In every organization for which I have worked, a pension plan was made available to me, but this is not always the case in charitable organizations. When no pension plan is offered to staff, they have no security for themselves or their spouse for their retirement years, except what is provided by the government. Some organizations provide so little, or plan so poorly, that what is available to some who have worked for less than full wages for most of their lives is a pittance, and they would not survive in today's economy except for the government support they receive.

There has been a move in the past few years to money purchase plans from defined benefit plans. The money purchase plans allow for the accumulated funds in the person's account at retirement to be used for purchasing an annuity. In most cases there is a provision for the retiree to shop for the best price available at the time. This is the type of plan available to organizations in the CCCC.

There are several choices regarding the employee/employer ratio of funds contributed to the pension plan. In some organizations the employer contributes all of the premium, in others the employer matches the contribution of the employee up to five percent of salary. The employee may choose to contribute more, but the employer's contribution will not exceed five percent. These are just some of the options available. Again, it is usually a budget decision as to the amount an organization can contribute.

Vacations

Everybody needs a vacation. In Canada the law requires employers to give paid time off for full time staff. My experience has been for the employer to provide two weeks vacation for up to three years of employment and three weeks after three years employment. Many organizations give four weeks after six or eight years employment.

There are many variations. For comparison, it is interesting to note that according to the U.S. Bureau of Labour Statistics, the average American full-time worker puts in a 40 hour week, gets 11 official holidays (statutory and other public holidays), and slightly more than two weeks of paid vacation. That is typical after five years on the job.

The British, on average, work 39 hours a week, get eight paid holidays and enjoy 25 days of paid vacation a year. The French, by law, work a standard week of 39 hours, have eight holidays and get 25.5 days of annual vacation. The Germans work a 38 hour week, get 10 holidays and have 30 days of paid vacation. Take your choice.

Company Vehicles

There used to be a substantial personal tax advantage to driving a company car. The Canadian government has taken away most of those advantages. However, to some extent, there is still some benefit. Many organizations provide a vehicle for the CEO and senior management. Vehicles may also be made available to staff who represent the organization to the public and are required to travel extensively as part of their responsibilities. Of course, for those driving company vehicles, the major benefit is not having to purchase a vehicle with their own money. In many cases a company vehicle will allow the family to have two vehicles at their disposal, which is a requirement today for many families. Driving a company car can have its drawbacks especially if the staff member leaves the organization and must then purchase his own vehicle. There is no doubt that driving a company car makes an employee think seriously about the cost of quitting.

If this type of benefit is being offered, the organization should have in place a very clear vehicle policy.

Special Events

Many organizations have a staff picnic (during working hours), a Christmas banquet (usually after working hours), and other occasions when they can offer staff a time together outside the office. World Vision also presents pins and plaques to staff to recognize their length of service. This is an annual event which takes place during a staff breakfast at the office. A staff committee arranges the event and a continental breakfast is served before the presentations are made. Also at this event, the Encourager Award is presented. This is given to the person who has been the greatest encourager amongst the staff during the year. Nominations for this award are made by the staff. The award is in memory of a deceased employee, who herself was a great encourager.

Flexible Hours

Flextime will not work in every organization, especially smaller ones where there are few staff. If the number of staff is large enough, it is a great way to increase morale, especially among working mothers.

Without going into a great deal of detail about the various options, it should be sufficient to say that there is a need to set core hours when all staff are required to be at the office. This is usually between 9AM AND 3PM. In a seven hour work day, with one hour for lunch, staff can arrive at work anytime between 7AM and 9AM and leave work anytime between 3PM and 5PM, usually on the hour or the half hour. For example, someone starting at 7AM would leave at 3PM; while someone starting at 7:30AM would leave at 3:30PM, etc. The manager in each department would be responsible to ensure that critical positions are covered at all times. It is the managers who monitor and approve staff hours.

Any organization that has introduced flexible hours has found it has been received wholeheartedly by the staff.

There are many ways to provide benefits to staff. Be creative.

STAFF PERFORMANCE EVALUATION

If an organization wants to retain its staff and do so in such a way that the employees feel that the organization cares about them, performance evaluations should be carried out at least annually on each and every employee, including the CEO. One of the worst things that can happen in an organization is to dismiss an employee for cause when the 'cause' had never been discussed with the employee. No employee, when they are being terminated for cause, should have to ask why. An annual performance evaluation will prevent surprises of this nature. The evaluation should be carried out by the manager, using a standard format. Forms can be prepared by the organization, or you can use one of the many that are available on the market. The procedure is simple. The manager and the employee each complete the form independently. They then compare and discuss their answers. Unresolved differences of opinion are noted and one copy of the form, signed by both parties and the manager's superior, is placed in the employee's file.

Not all organizations have formal performance evaluation procedures. Many managers feel that they can control the performance of staff, and will inform staff members when there is a problem. But that really does not do justice to evaluating staff. There is a misconception by many managers that evaluations are only performed to determine if the employee is doing a good job. Wrong. Evaluations will determine that, but evaluations also provide the opportunity to reward employees that are excelling. An evaluation should be one of the processes through which an organization determines annual salary adjustments.

If you have not looked seriously at this matter, you will not realize the several areas that should be considered when assessing an employee's performance. Do you examine how well they understand their responsibilities? The quality of work? The quantity of work? Work habits? Initiative? Interpersonal relationships? Supervisory ability?

What about training that might be required for your staff?

Have you discussed their career interests with them?

Evaluating staff performance cannot be accomplished by merely sitting with the employee and reviewing performance problems only when they become serious and only at a time convenient to the manager.

In one large charity, the managers could not agree on the evaluation process, although a standard form was being used. Some thought only the manager completed the form. Another thought that both the manager and the employee completed the form. Some were not sure who should complete the form! Some staff believed that it did not matter if they disagreed with their manager's assessment of their performance, as only the manager's remarks went into the Personnel file.

If your organization has no formal procedure for evaluating staff performance, it should be introduced. Then if you have a problem employee and no improvement is made in their performance over a reasonable period of time, you will have something in the files to show that there has been some communication with the employee about this over a period of time. It is one way to protect the organization against charges brought against it by a disgruntled, terminated employee. If the performance evaluation discloses some performance problem, what can be done?

PERFORMANCE IMPROVEMENT PLAN

A Performance Improvement Plan (PIP) is not just a way of saying to a poor performer, "If your work has not improved in the next two weeks, you had better start looking for another job".

Remember, the process of assisting a poor performer starts by identifying that there is a problem when the performance evaluation is carried out. There should be a section on the form for this purpose. It requires the manager to put into writing the need for an employee to be put on the PIP, and spells out the objectives.

The procedures are very simple. First, the need for improvement is identified. How that need will be met through the assistance of the manager or others is recorded, and a plan of action is determined, usually with a three month time limit. At the end of the three months another assessment is made. If the program has proven successful and the employee is performing satisfactorily, he is taken off the plan. The plan may be extended if progress is being made but more time is needed. If there is no hope in succeeding, then the employee is terminated.

One good thing about this plan is that the employee understands from the very beginning that he faces termination if he fails to measure up. There are no surprises.

I have seen this program work well with both clerical and middle management staff. Most poor performers appreciate the honesty of the organization in presenting them with the problem and giving them an opportunity to address it.

This program is not just a warning for the employee to improve. It says to him that the organization cares about his future.

Review the methods your organization is using to address poor staff performance. It is in the best interests of the organization to have some formal procedure in place.

One benefit of the PIP is its identification of the need for staff training.

TRAINING

When I worked for the Nestle company, I was a candidate for attending a business management school in Switzerland. This indicated to me that the company was interested in seeing me develop my management skills. Most companies offer training opportunities of some nature. Whether it's in-house training, attending outside seminars or funding for further education, there is a message sent from the organization to the employee – "we want you to learn more so we can give you more responsibility". That's the reason why companies invest in staff training.

Management must decide what funding the organization can set aside for this activity. Most organizations provide something. Training might involve sending a secretary on a one-day course, or maybe specialized technical training for computer programmers, or possibly training in Lotus 123 for the accountant so that the budget can be computerized. Available training funds must be prioritized to meet the greatest needs of the organization. There are at least two areas of training for which funds should be set aside – the development of interpersonal relationship skills and the development of management skills. I believe that poor performance in these two areas contribute more to staff turnover than any other reason.

Interpersonal Skills

Interpersonal relationships deal with how we get along with one another. In every organizations you can find tension between people.

One of the best courses I took while I was with World Vision dealt with the whole subject of interpersonal relationships. All of the management staff participated. It was frightening, to say the least. Discovering what kind of person you really are can be frightening. However, the course leader did say that there was no right kind of person. We discovered that we were all different, and that's why we act differently.

For instance, the Controller was "analytical". That's why he needs a list of at least ten reasons why you really need to spend that money. He also wants to make sure that every penny is accounted for on expense reports and that all receipts are attached. (Now we know why accountants are called 'bean counters'.)

Those working in fund raising are usually "expressive" types. That's why they don't like to take the time to fill out expense reports and attach all the receipts that the Controller wants.

Something I discovered about myself – I am an "expressive/amiable" type. It was pointed out that I like people (which is true). But it also confirmed something that I knew about myself, but had never had anyone identify. My type of temperament requires affirmation. I love it when someone tells me I've done a good job. I guess that's why I was always asking the boss if he liked what I presented to him. You know what I mean..."Here's the report you asked for. Does it look okay? Is there anything else you want added? Did the board say anything about my presentation to them yesterday?, etc., etc." All the time thinking to myself, just say "it looks good, Ken", and I'll be happy.

Well, I kept my position with World Vision for 15 years, so I guess I did something right. And my bosses were very good at giving affirmation.

The problem with many people, especially those who are responsible for directing the work of others, is that they do not know how to handle their staff properly. They lack basic skills in the area of interpersonal relationships making it imperative for organizations to allocate funds for training managers in interpersonal skills.

Management Skills

The other problem I have found in many organizations, is the lack of management skills in managers. So many problems within organizations today are caused by people being placed in management positions who do not know how to manage properly.

I have met managers who are not even clear about the management policies within their organizations. Many of them do not even know how to write a position description, and in many cases, do not have one of their own. There are those that have never been taught how to prepare a proper budget, yet have to submit one to the CEO every year.

The Oxford dictionary defines management as "conducting the working of a business, having effective control of a business". This is not what is being accomplished by some of the managers I know. There have been a multitude of books written on management, explaining what constitutes the traits of a good manager. We know they should be able to perform the basics – planning, leading, organizing and controlling. Do you see that in the managers in your organization, (or in yourself if you are a manager)?

The managers in many organizations are working managers. They perform technical work. If they are busy enough doing technical work, they do not have the time to consider planning, leading, organizing and controlling. Time is always the problem. Too much work to do. Not enough time to be a manager. So who suffers? The manager, the staff and ultimately, the organization as a whole. Everybody is frustrated. But the manager will have to find time when the frustrated staff quit and he has to replace them.

Another problem, in religious organizations particularly, is the manager who thinks it is not "Christian" to discipline, and this attitude applies even more so to termination. I know managers who have had problems in their departments for months, even years, and the response they frequently offer to disgruntled staff is – "keep praying about it – it will work itself out".

The inability of managers (and I mean those in authority up to the CEO) to manage properly, could be one of the major reasons why there is staff turnover in your organization.

This is reason enough to invest some time and money in training people in the basics of interpersonal relationships and teaching managers to manage. These should be priorities in every organization.

COMMUNICATING

To impart news.

We all want to be knowledgeable – it is human nature to have a "need to know".

A recent issue of Time magazine explained how 35 years ago, six students at Korea University in Seoul decided to deepen their understanding of the world while increasing their knowledge of English. They met to read Time magazine while translating it together. From this small beginning, thousands of members have been attracted to participate over the years, and similar groups have been generated in ten other universities, thus showing man's hunger for increased knowledge.

In every organization you find a difference of opinion between the board, the management and the staff, on who should have knowledge of what. There are those that think they have a right to know everything. There are those who think that too much (or too little) information on any matter could be dangerous. There are those that don't ever want to share anything (everything is "personal/confidential"). These problems will need to be worked out within each organization to best fulfil its needs. However, there is an inherent need within all of us to know what is going on. I don't mean this in a nosey way, but in a business sense of keeping staff informed for the benefit of the organization.

My first real exposure to good staff communications came when I worked with the Nestle company. There was a written communication circulated to staff throughout Canada on every staff appointment, promotion and termination. We always knew what was happening in the Personnel area.

There are a number of ways to keep staff informed of those things that have an impact upon them.

A staff newsletter is one way to communicate within an organization. News about the organization's activities can be included in this periodical, along with information about staff birthdays, hirings, departures, etc. Prepared by the Personnel Department or someone in a management position, it can be issued monthly. This is a good vehicle through which the CEO can share with the staff.

Most charitable organizations receive reports of their work and accomplishments. This material should be circulated to the staff to encourage them.

The use of a staff bulletin board is another good method of communicating. The activities of other organizations can be shared here as well but everything put on the board should be monitored by the Personnel Manager.

Periodic meetings with all staff should be held where management can share items of interest or concern. This also would provide an opportunity for the staff to meet visitors from overseas, or see the latest video or film about the organization's work. I have seen this type of forum used effectively by the CEO to answer staff questions.

There is also a need for the CEO to communicate regularly with the managers and the board must communicate regularly with the CEO. But our focus here is particularly directed to ensuring that good communications exist between management and staff. An informed staff is a happier staff.

A review of communications in a large charity recently elicited these responses from staff when asked how well they thought management was communicating with them (some were managers):

• "Communications today are much better than they used to be".
• "Materials are circulated to managers and then on to the staff, but only if the manager decides".
• "Reading material is available in various departments".

• "The information meetings every week are beneficial".
• "Department heads do not always share information with us".
• "There are not enough department meetings where managers can share with their staff".
• "Even the managers are not always informed of important matters".

RECOGNITION OF STAFF

Everyone likes recognition. The kind of recognition where the CEO gets Joe up in front of the staff to congratulate him for a job well done.

The management at McDonald's (the hamburger people) knew what they were doing for staff morale when they introduced the Employee Of The Month Award and displayed that employee's picture in the store.

Now there are different degrees of recognition, and the recognition that Joe receives obviously warrants it happening in front of all the staff. But just as effective is the recognition Mary might receive within her department. The point is, both Joe and Mary feel very good about their job and the organization because they have been chosen for recognition, whether it be in front of a large group or a smaller one.

Sometimes this recognition might involve the CEO taking someone out for lunch to show appreciation for a special effort. Or perhaps a staff member might be invited to a board meeting to have the board thank him for a job well done. Or maybe their picture could be published in the staff newsletter.

The Performance Evaluation process discussed earlier identifies staff who display superior performance. The most effective recognition in this case would be a salary increase. This merit increase is given in addition to the cost of living increase that all staff would receive. No special announcement here, but the employee is encouraged just the same.

Length of service awards are usually part of every organization's staff recognition procedures. In some organizations, staff that have been there for more than two years are called "long term employees".

Apart from the special cases, sometimes all it takes is a sincere "thank you". All staff like to know that the boss has recognized them and their contribution to the organization.

WHY DO STAFF LEAVE?

A recent revealing survey I conducted was based on the question, "Why do you think people leave the organization?" I received the following responses:

- "More money".
- "They are young people looking for something different".
- "Problems with their manager".
- "No opportunity for promotion".
- "Lost confidence in the organization".
- "Got fed up with their work".
- "Planned on being here for only a short time anyway".
- "Found a job better suited to their skills".

These answers are not unique. In most organizations a similar survey would probably reveal the same reasons.

A LACK OF LEADERSHIP CAN BE DEVASTATING

One of the most quoted reasons staff leave an organization involves a lack of effective leadership.

In one situation in which I was involved the organization had been without a Vice-President Finance for several months. The staff of 15 were being kept together under the leadership of the Finance Director, who was reporting directly to the President.

As acting Vice-President Finance my assignment was to pull the finance group together with the goal of putting some credibility back into the section while at the same time recruiting a permanent VP.

The staff felt that they were being blamed for everything that was going wrong in the financial areas of the organization. The board, management and staff in other departments were "on their case". When I arrived on the scene, several of the employees were already looking for other jobs. It only took a few days to realize that this talented group of people lacked one basic thing – a leader. They needed someone who could guide them, nurture them, encourage them and represent them as a Division to the rest of the organization.

I knew I had a challenge when I asked one staff member who she reported to. She sheepishly responded, "I'm not sure".

"Do you have a position description?", I asked.

"I'm not sure. I've never seen one", she replied.

Well, that was as good a place as any to start.

We took a few weeks getting the division organized – position descriptions, procedures, organizational chart etc., so that everyone eventually understood who reported to who. The more technical things began to fall into place fairly quickly, but I sensed other problems. Dissension among some of the staff in the division itself, and tension between finance staff and other staff in the organization. There was no team spirit. In fact, there was no spirit at all. The group had reached the point where they did not really care any more. How could I help these people recover their sense of self-worth? I arranged a staff retreat away from the office. In preparing for the day together, I asked each of them to submit their wish list to me anonymously. These were some of the comments I received:

• "Ken, may I speak honestly with you. I haven't been here very long and I don't want to say something that is not true. I enjoy all of the people here but the Department Manager. The people here in the Accounting Department work very hard. Most of us don't take breaks or a lunch hour and stay eight hours plus without claiming overtime. No matter how hard we try, he just isn't happy with us. He doesn't smile or say "good morning" or anything. We have to keep ourselves up for everyday battles because we have no support from him...He has called two meetings this year for the department. He doesn't care how we feel as a department or as people..."

• "I wish the Finance Department would be accepted by the rest of the organization. It seems that we always get the leftover copy machines, computers and other equipment. We need these just as much as everyone else to do our jobs".

• "I wish the organization would be open about what is going on. We need to be part of the vision. Perhaps then the rumour mill will be curbed and we will have a sense of security or at least enough info to allow us to be motivated...Would hire a strong leader who is permanent...that I and my colleagues know our job descriptions and can follow them..."

• "I wish the department could have more structured technical training..."

• "I wish the department would take a firm stand on their policies and procedures and work consistently on each procedure, instead of bending the rules and making exceptions".

• "We need the trust that only top management can give to us when we are making decisions..."

• "I wish the organization would refocus on what it is really all about...That the department would work more as a team. We do not get all the support we really need from top management".

As you can see, the staff expressed some legitimate concerns.

During the day together in a casual setting, we discussed some of the concerns they expressed in their notes to me. We talked about how we could build a team. Our agenda included such things as:

• lack of leadership
• lack of management staff
• lack of managerial skills
• lack of staff worth
• improving interpersonal relationships
• lack of organization and meeting deadlines

At the end of the day we all felt there was some new direction for the group. They felt affirmed and needed. They felt more like a team.

I share this story because it demonstrates what can happen to staff (in this case a division), when they lack strong leadership for any length of time. It's like a ship without a captain, or a football team without a quarterback. The ship will eventually run aground and the football team never wins a game because they consistently fumble the ball. Nobody is calling the plays.

Managing is not only directing people. It requires building a team that will feel good about their contribution to the organization.

I have only touched on a few of the factors affecting staff turnover. The staff attrition rate in charitable organizations can be as high as 15%-20%. This rate could be reduced considerably if management would devote some energy to implementing and improving upon the items mentioned in this chapter.

6

I'm Sorry,
But You're Fired!

The manager had asked the clerk to meet with her at 3 o'clock that afternoon for a performance review. The three month probation period was just ending and it was standard procedure to have such a review. The manager, who reported to me, had indicated that there were some performance problems and the probation period should be extended for at least another two months. I agreed. At 3:30 the manager came into my office.

"I just fired Susan", she said, angrily.

Before I could even ask what happened, she went on.

"She would not accept an extension of her probation period. She said she would rather quit so I told her she did not have to quit. She was fired".

I am not sure I would have handled the situation that way, but I think the manager and I would have reached the same conclusion. Not having been in the meeting, I was fairly certain that the discussion had been somewhat heated, and that bothered me. Not so much the outcome but the way it happened. It was not the way I would want any employee treated, especially if they were being terminated.

However, before I had too much time to reflect on the situation, the irate husband was in my office letting me know in no uncertain terms what he thought about this so-called "Christian" organization. The repercussions of that nasty encounter carried on for weeks. We had phone calls from the husband, the pastor and eventually, a letter from a lawyer. It is an understatement to say that this should never have happened.

But it did. And it still happens in many organizations.

This is not one of my favourite subjects, but neither are death and taxes, yet they are a reality. Staff get fired whether the company is for profit or non-profit. Although you may think that employees are treated differently in religious organizations, this has not been my experience. In fact, many religious organizations do not terminate their staff as humanely as some secular organizations.

Temper, Temper

Bill was a competent manager and had always handled his department well. But a situation developed that finally brought out the worst in him. He lost his temper and yelled at one of his staff members in front of the other staff.

Sally was experiencing some very dramatic personal problems within her family. Her work was suffering because of it. The situation had been going on for several weeks and Bill felt that he had to deal with it. Although he sympathized with her situation (according to her, even her life had been threatened), he did explain to her that she had to be at the office to carry out her duties to the best of her abilities. He could not let her continue to be absent as often as she had been during the past few weeks.

The situation deteriorated to the point that other staff members were now getting involved in her problems. Some were having to perform her work. Others felt that she was not being truthful. Tensions were mounting within the department.

After several more weeks of increasing pressure on Bill and his staff, Bill decided that Sally had to be terminated with a fair severance. It was determined that she could no longer do her job properly. This decision was not made lightly. But, at the termination meeting, Bill lost his cool. The details are not important, except to say that accusations were made and people were accused of lying.

In the heat of the discussion, Bill took the envelope which he had prepared for Sally and flung it across the table with these words, "You're fired! And the sooner you get out of this office, the better!"

I was shocked. This was so unlike Bill. He was normally a very gracious and kind person. But he broke. Unfortunately, he erupted in front of me and one other member of his staff. It was embarrassing. Sally burst into tears and I felt sorry for her.

After the initial shock wore off, I turned to Bill and admonished him for acting the way he had. It took several days for Bill to finally meet with me to discuss his actions and apologize for his behaviour.

This incident reminds us that even very good managers sometimes "lose their cool". But, if the manager is consistently fair and kind to staff, occasionally losing one's temper can be forgiven. If you are a manager with a temper that often erupts, you will probably have problems building a team spirit among your staff. There is a place for firmness in managing people, but shouting in a fit of temper has no place in management. Those who have a temper, should work at keeping it in check. You will be a more effective manager with a more supportive staff.

ACCOMMODATING INSTEAD OF TERMINATING

One of the worst things an organization can do is to accommodate staff that should be terminated. This is not being honest with the employee who can't carry out his work assignments. In this type of situation a manager may try to arrange a transfer for the problem employee to another department in order to provide suitable work. This is good, if it succeeds. But what if it doesn't? I have seen too many cases where employees have been moved around within an organization in an attempt to find something that they can meaning-fully do. I believe honesty with the employee is the best policy. Some organizations would never suggest an employee go and find another job but this is not fair to the employee or the organization.

Of all the situations that I have encountered, one I remember best involved an employee in a fairly senior position. As the organization grew, the structure was changed several times to accommodate this growth. This particular person was "left behind". To accommodate his loss of seniority, he was placed in several different roles over a period of several years: planning coordination, recruitment for over-seas personnel, assistant to the Personnel Director, special assistant to a Vice-President, and so on. I'm sure he must have come into the office some days wondering if he still reported to the same boss that he had the night before.

Eventually he found other employment on his own, but not until he had spent several frustrating years with the organization.

My policy has been to not play with people's lives and careers. If they are not contributing and cannot be placed in a meaningful position then suggest they make a career change.

PERFORMANCE IMPROVEMENT PLANS

There are a number of options within an organization to deal with employees who are not performing as they should.

If the organization had a Performance Improvement Plan (PIP) in place, as mentioned in the previous chapter, the employee who is facing termination would know in advance that his job was in jeopardy. No surprises. That's the way it should be.

One advantage of a Performance Improvement Plan is that it allows managers to document the problems they are having with employees. This is an integral and important part of the performance evaluation process.

THE TERMINATION MEETING

Here we are dealing with termination for just cause. The labour laws are such that all organizations need to document discussions with the employee prior to their termination. All discussions should be confirmed with the employee, in writing, with a copy placed in the Personnel files. It will save untold grief, both with the government, and/or lawyers, if the organization has documented everything relating to the employee's performance and the warnings he was given. This is an important point.

How do you handle the actual termination discussion? Should the manager do it alone? Should it be done by telephone? Should we send a letter to their home?

Usually when an employee is terminated for just cause, they already know they are being let go so there is not too much surprise and anger during the meeting. But, in all fairness to the employee, we should make it as painless as possible and ensure he leaves with a measure of respect and dignity.

Who attends the meeting is determined by the employee's level. If it is a junior position, usually the manager and the Personnel Director would be at the meeting. The more senior the level, the more senior those in attendance. The best approach is to have the immediate superior attend along with the Personnel Director. If there is no Personnel Director then the immediate superior, along with his superior, should be in attendance. I think it is always in the best interest of the organization to have two people involved in the meeting, if for no other reason than to be able to substantiate what is said.

It is my preference to have as much of the necessary documentation ready for the person who is leaving, such as the Unemployment Insurance form and final pay cheque. This avoids having to mail them to the employee or requiring him to return to the office to get them. The question of severance pay is usually determined by government regulation. However, I know that many organizations give more than is required.

Although I have been guilty of doing this myself, I recommend that you do not meet with the terminated employee at 4:00PM and tell him to clean out his desk and not return to work tomorrow. There are exceptions, of course, but most staff facing termination should have the privilege of saying good-bye to friends. If possible, give a dismissed employee at least two days to clear up their work and say their farewells.

LETTERS OF REFERENCE

More than once I have had to terminate someone for poor performance, and then have them ask me for a letter of recommendation. If anything good could be said about the person, I would gladly say it. But I am very careful what I might state in a letter about someone who has been terminated for just cause. A prospective employer could put you into a very embarrassing position if they called to verify the terminated employee's performance. Especially if they were to ask that favourite question, "Would you rehire this person?"

OUTPLACEMENT COUNSELLING

Depending on how senior the position is, many organizations now offer outplacement counselling for terminated staff. There is a cost involved, but it is a good way of assisting the employee to find another job. The circumstances surrounding the employee's termination would determine to what degree this counselling should be included in the severance package.

WORK REDUCTION, LAYOFF AND JOB SHARING

A reduction in the organization's income is another reason why staff may be terminated. Some organizations have written procedures to handle situations like this. Usually part time employees are the first to go, then full time staff according to seniority. However, there is also a need to identify critical positions that might be exempt from this standard progression. This may include positions in data processing, for instance. Senior management must decide what positions are untouchable due to the nature of their contribution to the organization.

Job sharing has been attempted in some organizations. I have had employees suggest that jobs be shared by several full time staff to avoid someone losing their job. If this is done, it can create some problems. For instance, some employees could not afford to take a reduction in pay as a result of reduced hours. Also, I have found that not all staff members support this approach as an alternative to laying off some of their co-workers. If there is not complete support, it will create tension within the organization. Several questions that might be asked include, "Why should long term employees be asked to sacrifice for those who have been with the organization only a short time", or "Why should an employee who represents the only income in the family take a reduction in salary to keep someone employed who has a spouse working full time somewhere else?"

LETTERS TO THE BOARD

There is one delicate situation that can develop when staff are terminated. A disgruntled employee may write to the chairman of the board and/or other board members. This has happened more than once in my experience.

The wise board member who receives such a letter will speak personally to the board chairman, and a wise chairman will speak to the CEO, and then let management manage! It can only cause grief when a board gets involved in staff dismissals.

In one such case, a terminated employee had some of the elders in his church contact the board. (One of the board members attended the same church.) What a disaster! The discussion went on for months but the employee was not reinstated.

EMPLOYEES ARE PEOPLE

Although organizations must terminate staff for just cause or otherwise, we must remember that the employee being terminated is a person. My relationship with many religious organizations constantly reminds me that terminated employees in these organizations are more than just people, in a sense they are brothers and sisters and should be treated as such. Managers should never let their heads rule their hearts.

We all like to think that the terminated employee will go quietly and cause no problems. But that does not always happen. Every organization must treat their employees as people, even those being dismissed, (or should I say, especially those being dismissed).

The Core Values statement that World Vision developed a few years ago says something very important about people:

"We value people. We regard all people as created and loved by God. We give priority to people before money, structure, systems and other institutional machinery. We act in ways that respect the dignity, uniqueness and intrinsic worth of every person – the poor, the donors, our own staff and their families, boards and volunteers..."

EXPERIENCES NOT EASILY FORGOTTEN

A number of incidents from my career have guided me in the way I now handle certain employee situations.

Odours

I liked Ted. He was a good worker and never really caused any problems for me. He met his deadlines and always asked for help if he had problems with the work. He would probably be promoted if he stayed with the company.

It all started when I peered up over my glasses one morning to see Mary standing in front of my desk. I had not heard her enter.

"What is it Mary?", I asked innocently, thinking that she had some problem with the accounting. I could see out through the glass partition into the large office where my staff were seated. It was one of those offices where everyone's desk was face to face in squares of four. (I never liked that arrangement because one person could sneeze on Monday, and everybody else had colds by Friday.) But what was odd was that several of the staff were looking into my office as Mary stood before me.

"It's Ted", was her simple response.

Oh, she's had an argument with Ted, I thought.

"Well, what seems to be the problem".

"He smells".

I wasn't sure I heard her correctly, so I hesitatingly asked, "What do you mean, he smells"?

With some boldness she went on, "The girls in the office asked me to come and speak to you about it. Something has to be done. He has terrible body odour and we can't stand working beside him any more".

Oh the joys of management! How do I tell Ted about his B.O? The next day, (I thought the girls could survive one more day while I thought of how to deal with this), I called Ted into my office. As he sat down, I thought "do I just blurt out, Ted, you have body odour"?

"What do you want to talk to me about, Ken?", he asked somewhat sheepishly.

So I proceeded very carefully to tell Ted that he was not using enough deodorant, if he used any at all! There were other things related to Ted's habits as well that had been mentioned to me. I laid it all out for Ted. He did not argue. He did not deny it. I think he was too ashamed to say much at all. But, he was back at his desk the next morning. I did not follow up on the complaints to see if they had been corrected. To Ted's credit, no more was said by either himself or the girls. Ted stayed, and was still working for the company when I left.

Marriage Problems and Performance

Sam had been having problems in his marriage for some time. I was not aware of this but his immediate superior was. His boss had spent a lot of time talking with him over a period of several months, trying to assist him in getting things right in his marriage. However, Sam's productivity was deteriorating. This problem was having a drastic effect on the department he managed.

Finally, during his annual review, Sam's boss faced him with his poor performance. It was going into the record that he needed to improve in several areas. Sam didn't appreciate the discussion. During the years he had been with the organization, he had always had good performance evaluations. He objected strongly to his boss's assessment and the case came to my attention.

After some deliberation over a period of weeks, it was decided that it was in his best interest and the organization's to give him a chance to improve. By this time his marriage break up was complete. His staff were very supportive of him but this caused problems between them and Sam's boss, who they felt was treating him unfairly.

Sam was happy that he would have an opportunity to prove that his work was not suffering because of his problem. Unfortunately, he failed. Within a few months Sam was told that he was not going to be kept on. We did all we could for him, but he was just not able to handle the work any longer. He left with some ill feeling toward the organization, but a fair severance package was worked out for him.

An interesting aspect of this case involved his staff, many of whom said that if Sam left they would go also. None did.

Sometimes Its The Good Ones That Have To Go

For several weeks I had not slept well. My wife finally suggested that I take action on this particular termination right away so I would stop fretting. This was one of those cases that bothered me more than others.

It all began when the organization decided to downsize a major division. This option had been discussed for several months and the dollar savings would be substantial. Because the division was my responsibility, it was my task to reduce staff in the division from eight to three. In this reduction, the Division Director would lose her job. I cannot recall ever having to terminate so senior a person before. Her seniority was only one of the tension – causing problems. The other one was related to the her performance. She was an excellent employee and had contributed much to the organization over the few years she had been on staff. I was not sure how to face meeting with her but I knew we had to meet soon. In fact, the meeting should have taken place already.

She was not being terminated for cause. Nor could I suggest she was being dismissed because of poor performance. So, I concluded that the best way to approach this was to face her with the facts. (The truth, and only the truth.)

I admit I was nervous when I arrived in my office that morning. She had a very professional and business-like demeanour. If only I could have blurted out, "We have to let you go because of the terrible way you run your division". But I could not. So, I bit the bullet and with some trembling in my voice said, "We are going to downsize your division, and unfortunately, we are eliminating your position".

Her response took me by surprise. "Oh, is that right"?

From that point on I spoke about the reasons behind this decision, assuring her that it had nothing to do with her, and that the organization would do everything possible to assist her in finding another job.

Beneath her outward calm an emotional volcano was building up. I could see it. Fighting back the tears she blurted out, "Did you know I'm pregnant"?

This was not my day! Having felt so bad about telling her about the job loss, this really added to my chagrin. It was like kicking someone when they were down.

That day is etched in my memory. It all worked out over the following weeks. She was offered out-placement counselling and a fair severance. She also assisted me in announcing to other staff in her division that they too were about the lose their jobs.

This had been a difficult situation for me to handle. It seems so much easier to terminate staff when you can build a case with evidence to show why they should leave. I appreciated this woman's attitude and assistance in making things easier for me.

I remember saying to my wife during this particular episode, "This is the one thing I really don't like about managing – having to terminate the good employees".

A TERMINATION CHECK LIST

1. There is nothing wrong with terminating staff.
2. Delay increases the problem.
3. Do not accommodate poor performers – be honest with them.
4. Use a Performance Improvement Plan.
5. Never terminate by mail.
6. Consider outplacement counselling.
7. Avoid board involvement.
8. Remember, you are dealing with people.

7
Did You Plan on Failing?

PLAN AH
    E
    A
    D

You have probably seen that sign on someone's desk. It's a great reminder of a very important principle.

A couple of years ago I decided to build a recreation room in the basement of our home and announced this to my family. After the laughter subsided, one of my children remarked, "Dad, you've never lifted anything heavier than a pencil. What does an accountant know about building"?

Knowing the importance of planning, I explained that before commencing, I was going to enrol in a night school course entitled "How To Finish Your Basement". I'll never forget that first night at school. The teacher was a carpenter. He asked if anyone would like to have the class of 20 students work on their basement. Three volunteered. The winner's name was drawn from a hat. Every Thursday for 8 weeks we met at his home and worked on building a room in his basement. By December I was ready.

Right after Christmas I went into my basement and began tearing the insulation from the walls. Construction had commenced, but not before the plan had been completed. When I started that work, I knew exactly what I had to do to accomplish my goal. Granted, I had lots of help from friends and the sales clerks at Beaver Lumber. By May, I had completed the job, not professionally, but adequately. My family was amazed at my accomplishment. When the kids were small, I couldn't even fix their toys. Now, when asked the secret of my success, I could speak out with confidence, "I planned it this way".

Like most people, I don't like planning or budgeting. We all have the same complaint – "I don't have the time". Most of us want to be doing, not sitting and thinking about what to do or how to do it.

In our personal lives we would never survive if we did not carry out some form of planning and budgeting. Unfortunately, those who do not take the time to budget find themselves in debt over their heads, scrambling to pay off credit card balances! But to go into debt is a plan in itself. So, we all plan, but we do not all budget. You may survive without a good plan, but survival is more difficult without a budget.

What Comes First?

To plan or to budget? Most organizations have budgets, but this doesn't mean they have any formal planning process. There are two basic plans – long range and short range. The long range plan looks ahead three or five years, and the short range plan concerns itself with the upcoming year. The long range plan is also referred to as the Management Plan and the one year plan is called the Operating Plan.

A plan should be prepared before a budget. However, most organizations decide how much money they will have and then plan on how to spend it. So, as we enter into this review of planning and budgeting we must recognize three things:

(a) Management in most organizations do not take the time to plan.

(b) Most organizations do not know how to plan properly.

(c) Most organizations determine how much money will be available and then plan how to spend it.

PLANNING

Planning Is A Process

Organizations need to make plans every year. It would be somewhat foolish to think that we could plan for five years and then wait for five years before we plan again. We need to be attuned to our needs on an ongoing basis. Since detailed plans become less accurate with time, the only alternative is continuous planning.

You have probably heard some of the most common comments about planning, such as:

"It is not a question of whether we will make plans or not. Not to plan is a plan in itself".

"Planning asks the question as to whether we will affect the future at random or with a purpose".

"If you don't care where you are going, any road will take you there".

"No one plans to fail, they just fail to plan".

Planning is a process, not a one time event. It is a cycle. You plan, you budget, you operate and measure against the plans and budgets, and you plan again.

Planning Takes Time

Most people in management would agree that planning is necessary. These same people would also agree that we do far less planning than we should. The difficulty is that planning takes time and time is a commodity that is in continual short supply. The enemy of planning is the tyranny of the urgent. Remember the last time you decided to do some planning? It just happened that at that very time someone on your staff demanded your attention on some emergency.

Extended periods of quality time are required if you are going to do effective planning. It will require the right mix of people, the proper environment and good preparation. Good planning is the result of good planning.

When was the last time you put an entry in your diary to set aside time for planning? Most of us will not take the time unless we consciously set it aside. At the same time if the CEO is not giving leadership in the planning process, other staff members can't be expected to be motivated and excited about it.

The Players

It is incorrect to think that the board and the CEO should decide where the organization is going in the next few years and how it will reach its goals. Wherever possible, the planning process should involve the people who are going to do the work. Every manager should be involved in the planning process. This is a basic dimension of management work. Every manager's position description should contain comments on Planning, Leading, Organizing, and Controlling. If your managers' position descriptions do not include these activities, I suggest you write them in. Planning is the responsibility of management – all management.

It is also necessary to recognize that certain people are better at long range planning than others. Some people just do not like to plan. I have found that not all managers are able to contribute effectively to the long range plans of the organization, even though they are responsible for the one year plan in their own area. While all managers must be involved in developing the one year operating plan for their department, these same managers may not be contributors to the longer range plans of the organization. The long range planning process requires people who can think about and see the larger picture. More recent long range planning sessions in which I have been involved have included one or two members of the board, the CEO, some selected management staff and an outside consultant. The participants may change each year.

The Planning Context Meeting

Spending a day brainstorming can result in some wonderful "think tanks". In my experience we always looked into the future and discussed issues that we thought might impact upon the organization, such as, the speed of technological changes.

Another interesting discussion involved personnel and the difficulties of obtaining properly trained staff in the future who were committed to the organization. One major issue has always been whether the staff we would require in three to five years would be available, and if not, what should be done now to plan for this possibility?

Other areas discussed might include the economy, the effects of various legislation, increased pressures on charities with respect to accountability and how to meet these demands.

One good approach to any discussion of the future, is to look at the

assumptions that might be made about the next few years. For instance, some questions asked in our meetings included:
- How long will there be a continuing need for our programs?
- From whom can we expect the greatest support for our programs?
- What can we assume about the stability of the organization with respect to its leadership? What if there is a different management and board? Will these changes affect the ethos and key objective of the organization?
- Do we expect our organization to grow in size, especially in the area of funding?
- What will be the impact of inflation?
- What do we expect to happen to other organizations with objects similar to ours?
- Will the present organizational structure still be viable and in place three years from now?

From considering these and similar questions, we developed strategic direction statements such as:
- Cashless Society: The organization will provide donors with the capability of forwarding funds using the latest technology and we will spend these funds using this same technology.
- Technology: The organization will utilize contemporary technology in the area of communications.
- Contingency Planning: Contingency plans will be developed and in place to enable the organization to respond to external and internal environmental factors.
- Service and Assistance To Other Agencies: The organization will provide to other agencies upon request, expertise that it uses in management, financial and data processing areas.
- Human Resources: The organization will develop and maintain its human resources to the degree that they function efficiently and effectively.
- Internal Financial Options: The organization will be aware of and have in place the latest financing techniques available to enable us to have the maximum cash flow possible for our programs at all times.
- Size: Funds raised by the organization will reach X number of dollars by 1995.

The important thing to remember in all this is that the planning process starts with developing a context in which to plan. This is the purpose of a typical planning day. During this time one item that should be discussed onto which all other discussion must hinge, is the Mission Statement or Key Objective.

Key Objective Of The Organization

Every organization should have a Mission Statement. In fact, every organization does have one. They just have not taken the time to formulate it into a full-blown Mission Statement and put it into print. What's so important about the Mission Statement?

• It gives the organization a reason for existing.

• It helps place boundaries around the activities of the organization, defining what will be done and what will not be done.

• It describes the goals of the organization and how it is going to meet those goals.

• It acts as the hook on which the primary objectives of the organization can be hung.

• It helps to form the basis for the ethos of the organization.

It is critical to know why the organization exists and what its Key Objective is before you formulate plans on how to meet that objective.

The Long Range Plan

This is the Management Plan and usually covers the next three to five years. I remember a time, not long ago, when the long range plan could look forward 10 years, but with the world changing so rapidly in so many areas affecting business, this in no longer practical. Most organizations are now only planning for three years into the future.

Long range planning is quite different from short range planning. It provides the context within which short range planning is done. The long range plan can be considered to be:

• an attempt to make better decisions today in light of tomorrow's expectations.

• an attempt to focus on the purposes of the organization and to support them with adequate goals.

• a process.

• the task of top leadership.

• risk-taking decision making.

Once the long range plan is completed using the assumptions and future contexts that have evolved from strategy meetings, this

Management Plan will provide the foundation for formulating the Operating Plan.

The Short Range Plan

This plan includes those items in the long range plan that will take place in the coming year, and for which the organization must not only plan but must also budget. Known as the Operating Plan, it involves only those goals that are reachable during the current year. The preparation of the Operating Plan is not difficult if the Management Plan has been completed properly.

Managers plan their activities for the coming year from the long range Management Plan. This is where most organizations run into problems. They do not let their managers plan. They expect them to budget but don't often involve them in the planning process. Even though the managers may not have been involved in the development of long range plans and the context in which the plans are prepared, they should be involved as much as possible in preparing their own Operating Plan.

Getting Started

(a) You have to start with yourself. As a leader you must determine what you want to do and where you want to be in one year, three years, at the end of your lifetime. Write down your own goals in action-oriented and measurable terms. You cannot lead other people in defining their goals, if you do not know your own.

(b) State your idea of the basic purpose (Key Objective) of your organization and then write some three year goals for it. Three years from now, how is your world going to be different because of what you and your organization have done?

(c) Consider what kind of an organization and what kinds of people are needed to accomplish these tasks. Wherever possible, make all organizational groupings around tasks, not functions.

(d) Establish goals which will capture the allegiance of your group.

(e) Bring together key people who can lead others. Ask them to start dreaming and thinking with you about what the organization should accomplish in three years.

(f) Bring other people into the process early on. Perhaps you could arrange a planning retreat by departments or other groupings. Remember the principle of goal ownership: "Good goals are my goals and bad goals are your goals".

(g) Prioritize the many good ideas you will receive.

(h) Determine the steps required to accomplish these goals.

(i) Estimate the cost in people, dollars and facilities.

(j) Assign specific people to the task.

(k) Communicate your goals in every way possible.

Remember, you are in a process. Every year, the situation will change. New goals will have to be set.

Fran Tarkenton, the well known NFL football quarterback who played for the New York Giants and Minnesota Vikings and is now a business consultant, has stated in his book *Playing to Win:*

"If you always wait until the right time or the good times to start, you will wait all of your life".

"If you let the past dictate the future, you will never go anywhere".

"You win by trying, not standing around".

I like this one:

"When all is said and done, more is said than done. Make it happen!"

Having established a good planning process, we can now look at how we will spend our money.

BUDGETING

Money In Envelopes

"Do we have any money left in the food envelope, dear?", was a question asked frequently in our household during the early days of marriage. The response would be something like this.

"No honey, but why don't we take some out of the Hydro envelope and replace it next payday?"

"But dear, we did that last month. I think we can use some money out of the Insurance envelope".

This was our simple attempt at managing our money. We had envelopes for everything; hydro, insurance, groceries, mortgage, clothing and even one for dinner out once in a while. What we were attempting to do was to make sure we did not spend money we did not have so we could pay our bills when they came due. I found it easier in those days to account for our money by having it separated in envelopes and stored in a metal box in my clothes closet. We always knew how much money we had. Most importantly when bills came due the funds were there to pay them.

This is really what budgeting is all about – making sure the funds are available to meet the operating demands as they fall due. This holds true for both home and business.

The Canadian Institute Of Chartered Accountants has defined a budget as, "A detailed estimate of future transactions, either in terms of quantities, or money values or both, designed to provide a plan for and control over future operations and activities".

Monty McKinnon, in his book *Money Management For Busy People* states, "Budgets are important. They are a practical demonstration of a plan and planning is an important principal". He is speaking here to individuals. But the same principals apply to organizations.

Like planning, budgeting is something for which most managers have little or no time. In a busy organization, everyone has daily tasks to attend to. When do managers get time to budget? They have to make the time. All of us would agree that budgeting is important and must be done. It is,

(a) a reflection of goals,
(b) a forecast of need,
(c) one measurement of progress toward goals,
(d) an indicator of success.

We are not going to discuss the various methods of budgeting. Most of us know what a budget is and how to prepare one. But I would like to comment upon a couple of the aspects of budgeting mentioned above. For instance, what do we mean when we say a budget is a reflection of goals?

A REFLECTION OF GOALS

Did you note that I said it was a reflection of goals? That means that the goals have been set before the budgeting process, not after. So we take the Operating Plan and now calculate the cost of accomplishing the things we plan to do next year. How do we do that? Well, in many organizations, managers like to take the previous year's spending and increase it by a certain percentage. That is not a solid basis on which to budget. Instead, we have put goals in place (or we should have), then we price them or apply dollars towards each goal. This will require some thought on the part of managers.

For example, what are the goals of an Accounting Department? We could list several, such as:

• To enhance the information given to management and to improve financial controls by reducing the time required to prepare monthly financial reports.

• To develop an automated system of cash forecasting and analyses to facilitate the investment of surplus funds in order to maximize interest yields.

• To provide training and development programs for the accounting staff.

Considering the Accounting Department's goals, the manager would prepare a budget based on meeting those goals.

The goals of the fund raising department should be developed first. The departments that support the organization administratively are directly affected by the activities of those involved in fund raising. The goals and the budgets of departments such as Accounting, Personnel and Data Processing will also be determined by the goals of the fund raising department. Note that I did not say the administrative goals and budgets are determined by the amount of funds being raised. **Money should not drive the planning process.** For instance, how funds will be raised may directly impact on data processing requirements. Perhaps there will be a new approach to raising funds such as putting an insert into the receipt envelope sent to donors. If this is to be prepared by the Data Processing Department, then its budget will be impacted by this decision, and the goals for that department should include this increased activity.

In every sense, the budget is a reflection of goals, even though ultimately it will be influenced by the income projections. It is important to remember that the budget is prepared on the basis of what an organization wants to do, and will be adjusted to what the organization can do once the dollars are projected. This gives management the opportunity to make adjustments to the plan in a rational way. It is always better to be pro-active than reactive.

Another important facet of the budget is that it forecasts need.

A FORECAST OF NEED

For most non-profit organizations, continuing operations are determined by the ability to identify needs and purposes, which are then communicated through the budgetary process as the reasons for securing the required funding. The information provided by this process assists in achieving an optimum use of available resources to meet the organization's goals.

Problems occur when management has not clearly communicated the needs of the organization when requesting managers to prepare their budgets. Management must be sure that everyone involved in budgeting knows what activities are being planned for the coming year. In this way the managers will be able to determine what they need to meet the demands that will be placed on them. For instance, a manager should be able to justify staff additions by stating to management, "If we are going to increase income by 10% next year I will require three additional staff". If this can be substantiated, then provision should be made in the budget to hire the staff. Justification is the key word here. Every manager should be required to submit his budget with justification for each item.

I like to approach budgeting by reviewing every expense item yearly, regardless of how much was spent the previous year. Justification for increasing any expense should not be determined on the basis that if income increases by 10% then costs will increase by some proportional amount. Managers must review every expense item each year and justify the expenditure for the next year. This is what is often referred to as "zero-base budgeting". This method of budgeting suggests that existing programs are maintained only after they have been justified in relationship to other available options. The concept of zero-base budgeting stems from the concern that the traditional budgeting approach simply reflects "add-ons" to the past year's expenses. Unfortunately, "adding on" is the method utilized by many managers. It is a simple method of budgeting, but it is not recommended.

One definition of zero-base budgeting explains it as:

"A management system whereby each manager must prepare a 'decision package' for each activity or operation, and this package includes an analysis of cost, purpose, alternative courses of action, measures of performance, consequences of not performing the activity, and benefits. Managers must first identify different ways of performing each activity – such as centralizing versus decentralizing operations, or evaluating the economy of in-house print shops versus commercial printers. In addition, zero-base budgeting requires that managers identify different levels of effort for performing each activity".

If the 'wants' are eliminated and only the 'needs' make it into the budget, these more accurate projections will allow management to determine the cost of reaching the goals set by the organization for the coming year.

Let us examine some of the major cost areas in a budget.

Fixed Assets

We all have difficulty determining "need" from "want". The old typewriter is about to die but it may have another year of life in it. The manager includes a new typewriter in his budget. The question is, does he need a new typewriter or does he just want a new typewriter? He probably has a good argument for a new one. But if funds are not available, the request will be denied because the old one still works. This brings us to the question of the degree of need. It would be desirable to have a new one, but maybe we can get by with the old one for another year. The manager has a "need" and a "want", but availability of funds dictates the action taken, which may be denial of the request.

The Fixed Asset budget should be prepared separately from the operating budget. Some years ago it was often suggested that if approval could not be obtained for the purchase of a new fixed asset, it should be leased. The cost of the lease would become part of the operating budget and would be less likely to be scrutinized by a board. (Boards always closely examine the fixed asset additions in a budget.) Generally accepted accounting practice requires that any fixed asset leased with a view to purchase at the end of the lease be treated as a "capital lease". As such, they become part of the fixed asset budget and are depreciated as if they had been purchased outright at the time of acquisition. There is no longer any budget advantage to leasing fixed assets as opposed to an outright purchase when it comes to accounting treatment.

What minimum cost level should be used to determine if a fixed asset should be depreciated or written off in its entirety in the year of acquisition? This depends on the size of the organization and the value of the asset. In many cases, fixed assets costing less than $500.00 would be totally written off in the year of purchase, with those exceeding that value being depreciated according to rates established by the organization. Some organizations choose to write off all fixed assets in the year of purchase. Certain information would have to be maintained for insurance purposes. When I began working for Nestle I found several small cost items in their fixed asset inventory, including a $50. shovel. These smaller value items just cluttered up the inventory. The cost of keeping a record of them exceeded the value of the assets themselves.

A good system should be put into place that will allow for the monthly monitoring of fixed asset purchases against the budget.

Personnel

Adding staff to any organization is expensive. You are not just impacting salary cost but also related benefits, which can amount to another 10% to 12%. You must also consider the furniture, supplies and other equipment a new staff person will require. However, when assignments are not being completed, a manager is going to request more staff. When an organization cannot afford to add people, what options are there?

I like to review current staff productivity and priorities. If there are staff that are not producing up to expected levels, then they should be evaluated and given an opportunity to improve. One of the worst things an organization can do is to add staff to do the work of present staff who are not performing well.

Examine the work being performed. Are there tasks being carried out within the organization that are not critical to reaching its goals? Budget time offers a wonderful opportunity to ask managers to justify the work being done in their departments. Force them to justify additional staff. I would ask them to prepare a "Justification Report" for additional staff requests. I remember one budget year when requests for additional staff were reduced by 50% when managers were told they could not hire staff unless they could provide reasonable justification. This more restrictive approach may require managers to change the scope of certain jobs within their departments. Many organizations perform the same tasks in the same way for years without review. Staff should not be added until such a review is carried out.

Some managers hire consultants as a means of getting around management's refusal to approve the hiring of additional staff. Consulting costs are not salary costs but most boards require an analysis of these costs, thereby reducing the possibility of using this method to circumvent the denial of salary cost increases.

Boards get excited when they see high staff numbers. The number of staff is not as critical a factor as the salary dollars being spent.

If management can keep within the dollar budget, they should be able to use whatever staff numbers they require. Once the salary and benefit budget is approved, I believe in letting management operate within that budget by using full time, part time or volunteer staff. Management must remember, however, that staff require space, furniture and supplies and must ensure that these costs are factored into the budget.

At World Vision we established a percentage of cash income as the criteria for salary costs. Direct salary costs were not to exceed 10% of cash income in any year. This rule of thumb guideline allowed management to utilize staff as the needs dictated and to add staff when necessary as long as the guideline was maintained. If income rose substantially over projections, staff could be added to meet the demands of increased activity. The number of staff was not the issue but only the salary costs as a percentage of income. Management was able to use part time staff where necessary, but these costs were included in the salary budget. Each organization would have to determine a reasonable income/salary cost ratio for their unique situation.

We must also recognize that in a time of decreasing income the organization would be required to reduce staff. The use of part time staff and volunteers allows for "downsizing" quickly. Job sharing by full time staff is another approach to reducing salary costs. But as mentioned earlier, it is not recommended.

Travel

Many organizations require an substantial travel budget. Travel costs can be defined in two areas, domestic and overseas. This is important for organizations that have program activities outside of Canada. I like to keep the costs separate because overseas travel costs can be considered program costs rather than administrative or fund raising costs. Costs related to travel within a reasonable distance of the office are usually charged to the automobile expense account.

The board should have a travel policy which defines the number of trips allowed by staff in any given year and the class of air travel. Management should be required to outline travel plans for the budget year and report monthly against those plans. It is not uncommon for boards to require an explanation of what will be accomplished on each trip. Some staff see travel as a job benefit. But the glamour of travel soon wears off although it is exciting to visit overseas projects.

Unless justification can be made for this travel it should not be approved. This applies to both board and staff travel.

ONE MEASUREMENT OF PROGRESS TOWARD GOALS

One of the major problems with respect to budgets is to ignore them once they are in place. There is no reason to budget if you are not going to monitor actual expenses against that budget. What reason is there for setting income and spending guidelines if nobody ensures they are being met?

To ensure that budgets are an effective control device and management tool, there are several things that must be in place:

• **There must be someone in the organization that knows how to budget.** I have seen many organizations that do not have accounting expertise in place. Budgeting by non-financial people can be a disaster!

• **A proper accounting system must be in place.** Many organizations do not have adequate accounting systems. It is difficult to make effective use of budgets if the financial records do not provide the detail required for proper monitoring.

• **Use a meaningful report.** The amount of detail required by each organization will differ. A report should be developed that will allow for the proper monitoring of each income and expense item. There can be many variations to this report. The minimum information should include:

Current month	- actual
	- budget
	- variance
Year to date	- actual
	- budget
	- variance

You can include other information in this report depending upon your needs and the capabilities of the accounting system. This additional information might include such things as Amount Remaining In Budget, Projected Spending For Year, Previous Years Actual, Variances (with percentages), and so on. Develop the report to meet your needs.

• **Issue a monthly report.** Comparing income and spending with projections must be done at least on a monthly basis regardless of the organization's size. If I were on the board of directors, I would want to know the financial state of the organization every month. Also, in order to make adjustments in spending, every manager should know at least monthly what variances there are between actual spending and projections.

• **Issue the report to those who need it.** Every manager responsible for the spending in his department should receive a regular report on that spending. The CEO would receive a full report covering the whole organization. The board would usually receive a condensed report, as they may not be interested in departmental detail. However, this would be dictated by the size of the organization. I always issued a full detailed report to the Treasurer and discussed it with him. Often, I would send a copy of the report to the auditors for their information and comment.

• **Provide necessary commentary.** I call this a Variance Report. This provides an explanation of major variances in actual income and spending in relation to budgeted amounts. If you do not want to comment on small variances, a range should be set that allows for small variances without comment. In some organizations any variance that exceeds 10% requires comment.

• **Ensure that all questions are answered.** Managers must be required to give explanations for variances. It is only through this process that management can make meaningful decisions. A small variance may become serious overspending a month or two later. A small drop in income in one month may indicate a trend for the year.

AN INDICATOR OF SUCCESS

We should not assume that reaching or exceeding income projections is the only means of measuring success, or that maintaining spending within budget is a good reason for managers to boast about how well they have performed. To measure performance, the organization and its management require much more than just a review of financial results.

The budget can be used to determine how successful the organization was in reaching its goals for the year. In most non-profit organizations this success is measured by the level of income, as the key objective of most charities is to raise funds for its programs.

But the success of the organization ultimately becomes the responsibility of the CEO who has to "make it happen". The CEO will answer to the board for those missed projections or any overspending.

The success of the CEO is greatly affected by the success of the managers. If they manage well and maintain spending within set limits, their success becomes the CEO's success.

The CEO and the Chief Financial Officer are ultimately charged with the responsibility of monitoring financial results and determining what organizational changes must be made to ensure success. If income is below projection, adjustments must be made to spending. Conversely, if income is above projection, increased spending might be necessary.

It is a management team effort and the team must meet frequently to ensure success.

Budgeting measures the success of the organization in reaching its financial goals and thereby measures management's performance. Boards compliment successful managers and CEOs but ultimately remove the unsuccessful.

CONCLUSION

If the budgeting process is not effective in your organization, get help! Some organizations have had to cease operations due to improper or inadequate control over their finances.

Planning and budgeting are critical to the success of any organization, regardless of its size. These important processes may determine not only how effective your organization is in reaching its goals, but whether it has a future.

8

Aerodynamic Pens, Removable Offices and Space Age Chairs

The room was small and windowless. Along the length of two walls were hundreds of files in old metal cabinets. (You know the type – those sickly green ones which are usually dented and only one of the four drawers works properly). The lighting was inadequate. A black dial telephone sat on one of the desks. Actually, the room was really just a closet converted to office space, at least that's what went through my mind. Even if I could not see the rest of the world, I knew I wouldn't be alone for they had managed to jam three other desks into this area which was no larger than a newsstand on a street corner.

This was my first work space. Having just graduated from high school, I was beginning my apprenticeship with a medium sized firm of Chartered Accountants in downtown Toronto. I was not about to complain about my work environment. In fact, I didn't know what a work environment was! Give me a desk, a chair, and enough light, and I was ready. (The chair, by the way, was one of those old wooden office chairs, not the modern spring seated type with the adjustable backs that let you work all day and not even know you are sitting down.)

This is the way it was when I started to work in a business office. As an auditor, I spent considerable time in clients' offices. Some of them also provided less than adequate furniture and a proper environment for their staff. I have worked at a desk in the middle of a hardware store; in a feed mill where an inch of dust covered everything, including the accounting records; on a coffee table in the living room of a client; and in a veterinarian office in the midst of caged animals. But you can adjust to anything when you know it's only a temporary assignment.

How much importance should organizations place on the work environment? The specialists will tell you that it is extremely important. You certainly do not have to convince most managers that proper facilities will make employees more productive.

In this chapter we will look at some of the aspects of office facilities that an organization should consider. This includes not only the environment itself, but how to move an office from one location to another. Consideration is also given to whether an organization should rent or own their facilities. Also, what is the impact on staff when an office moves a considerable distance from its present location? One of the most debated issues today is how organizations should handle the challenges of providing a proper work environment for their staff.

ADDITIONAL SPACE REQUIRED

Every organization has an office in which it carries out its administrative functions. It may be in a home or in premises of its own, sometimes owned, sometimes leased. Wherever the organization has a desk, a telephone and a mailing address it has an office. A mailing address is required for proper registration of the business, a box number is usually unacceptable. I favour a street address for charitable organizations because it gives them more credibility. This is true especially for newer ones. I always shy away from charities that want my money but do not have a street address where I can actually visit.

You may discover you need additional space when you suddenly realize that there is nowhere to put the new employee that starts on Monday. Hopefully, you will have planned properly and have allocated the required space.

Fortunately, my experiences have always involved well planned-in-advance moves. Some organizations do not plan ahead and then have to scurry around to find the space they need. This can be a real problem, especially if your present premises are locked into a long term lease. Trying to sublet under pressure is not easy or recommended. Terminating a lease in advance of expiry date can be expensive.

In 1975 Nestle moved from their location of many years on Carlton Street in Toronto, across from Maple Leaf Gardens, to their new headquarters at Eglinton and Don Mills Road. It was a well-planned move. As the new eight floor building was under construction, the old location was listed for sale or lease. (It remained vacant for a long time after the move and has since been demolished.) During construction the interior designer worked with us as we determined office and department locations, furniture requirements, etc. It was a major undertaking, covering a span of nearly a year. We finally moved in April 1975. The project had not been without its problems or pressures, as was apparent from the fact that the VP in charge of the project was on medication before construction ended. There were, however, some critical factors that made this project a success:

• The requirements for additional space had been identified well in advance of the need.

• Professional assistance was obtained when the expertise did not exist within the organization, (eg. interior design consultant).

• Someone in senior management acted as project coordinator, through whom all decisions were channelled and to whom all outside parties, such as contractors, related.

• Funds for the project were available.

Many other factors enter into a project of this scope, but the above points are fundamental to the success of any office move.

Within two years of the Nestle move, I found myself involved in another similar project with World Vision Canada, having joined the organization just a few weeks after the Nestle move.

World Vision was running out of space in their Scarborough location. Their leased premises had been enlarged to a maximum capacity of 11,000 square feet. No expansion space remained in the present location and the board had undertaken a study to determine where to relocate. Two options were being considered – the east end and the west end of Toronto. The board had already decided that the organization's headquarters should remain in the Toronto region.

A major Canadian realty company was engaged to study the options and come up with a recommendation. Several factors were included in this study: future development plans for the region, land costs, population growth, proximity to the airport, public transportation, etc. Each factor had a value placed upon it based on its importance to the decision. For instance, being near the airport was not as important as having public transportation for the staff.

The study recommended Mississauga as the best choice and the organization is still located in that city on the western border of Toronto.

Before we look at aspects of the actual relocation we should re-emphasize the factors that make any move a success:
• The need for additional space has been identified well in advance.
• Professional advice has been sought where required.
• Someone in senior management will act as project coordinator.
• The financial requirements of the project have been arranged.

Once the decision to relocate has been made, we should examine how best to accomplish it.

THE MOVE

Regardless of the organization's size, there are certain planning elements that must be considered well in advance. In any office relocation, staff needs must be of paramount importance.

We surveyed the staff through a questionnaire to determine how many of them would remain with the organization when it moved to Mississauga. The results were somewhat predictable. Those that would remain were (a) those who had transportation and could drive to the new location and (b) those who would move to the west end of Toronto.

Compensation was provided for staff to relocate their living accommodations which covered basic moving costs up to a set maximum amount. Only one staff member had to sell his home east of Toronto and in this case short term financing was provided.

Only 10 of the staff of 60 did not remain with the organization and a local church in Mississauga provided facilities for interviewing candidates to fill the vacated positions.

Even before the move, however, certain staff considerations were developed:
• Involve staff early in the planning process. Keep them informed of the project's progress. Answer their questions.

• As early as possible, determine how many staff will relocate so the organization can plan for their replacements.

• Develop a plan to compensate staff who will face personal moving costs.

• As much as possible, involve the staff in the selection of new furniture, colours, etc. This is usually handled through a staff committee. Be careful to avoid delays in decisions caused by too many opinions. Consensus is always a nice way to make decisions, but management should have the final say.

• Consider what components are necessary in the new environment to provide the most comfortable workplace for staff.

THE OFFICE ENVIRONMENT

Organizations have taken major strides in improving office environments since my early days in a badly lit office. During the 70's and 80's, companies became aware of a new approach to office interiors known as ergonomics or "the total office environment". No longer could an organization meet the needs of their staff by simply providing new furniture, now the total office environment had to be examined. This included furnishings, of course, but now particular attention was given to lighting, noise levels, colour schemes, whether to use ceiling to floor walls or movable panels, and where to place the plants that were now part of any office interior.

This was progress. It took us out of the dark ages. For years I have had this picture in my mind of the accountant with the green eye shade, sitting on an old wooden stool, writing with a pen that needs to be constantly dipped into an ink bottle. But we are a long way from those days. Unfortunately, many organizations are still operating in the dark ages. They may have more modern chairs, having replaced the old stools, and the accountant is probably using a ball pen. But the rest of the environment within the office has not changed substantially.

Let's look at some of the environmental factors that organizations should consider when moving to new facilities or modernizing their present facilities.

Furniture

Some organizations pride themselves on being able to obtain the best deals in used furniture. Have you ever wondered why this used furniture is available? It's usually because the previous owner found something better. I'm not saying that used furniture should not be acquired and sometimes the price is too good to pass up. But, be especially careful when purchasing chairs because it is a known fact that back problems are caused by badly constructed office chairs. What is the sense of acquiring used chairs if the savings are eaten up by lost productivity because staff members must visit their chiropractor three times a week?

Furniture manufacturers have spent millions of dollars developing chairs that minimize back problems and cause little or no strain. Investing in a good new chair will pay dividends. Consider this the next time you are looking at those bargains.

Partitions vs Walls

To me, an office has four walls that reach from the floor to the ceiling. Until World Vision moved to Mississauga, that was my office environment. In their new facilities, World Vision decided that the more economical and modern approach to office efficiency was the 'open concept'. Instead of walls, partitions of various heights and colours were used. Nobody in the new building had an enclosed office, not even the CEO. There were, however, enclosed meeting rooms and a board room.

Although I favoured the open concept for general offices, a lack of enclosed offices created some concerns for several managers. Although a sound masking system had been installed in the building and the partitions were 'sound absorbing', these factors did not eliminate the problem of sound travelling beyond the "offices".

Shortly after moving into the new facility, I was speaking on the telephone in my office. During the conversation my Accounting Manager entered the office, placed a file on my desk and whispered, "You may need this. It has the figures in it that you are discussing with Mr. Jones".

My conversation had been heard by my manager on the other side of the screen. Confidentiality no longer existed in my area. If telephone conversations could be overheard, it was likely that conversations during meetings in my office could also be overheard.

Now I realize that most people do not purposely listen in to other people's conversations, but I have heard enough comments from staff about items they heard over a screen, to realize that it happens.

My preference is an enclosed office because of the privacy it provides. Very often, meetings in my office involved discussions related to salaries, staff, and other confidential matters, some of them pertaining to board activities. It was not until an addition was put on the building a few years later that an enclosed office was provided for me. Not everyone agreed with me on this issue. In fact, the CEO continued to operate in an open office but then it was somewhat isolated from the general office area so noise was not a factor.

There is no doubt that having an open concept office has saved World Vision thousands of dollars over the past few years because of the ability to change the office configuration with little effort and without removing walls. It is certainly a recommended approach as long as enclosed areas are provided for managers who require them.

Another negative factor regarding partitions involves the eyesore they can become when people begin to use them for their own personal bulletin boards. It was the rule of the day when World Vision moved into their new office that nothing was to be pinned or taped to the partitions. There were several good reasons for this – it would avoid damaging the partitions, it would not destroy their sound absorbing effectiveness, and the general office decor would not be destroyed. The staff seemed to understand this reasoning and complied, at least initially. Then slowly screens became home to an odd piece of paper or a picture, or maybe a small calendar. Within a few months staff had forgotten or did not care about the reasons for keeping the partitions clear. I was hard pressed to understand why little Billy's hockey schedule had to be in front of mother at the office all day, but there it was.

I used to be very adamant about this issue. However, as time went by it became apparent to me that these work areas become very much a personal environment for each staff member. This is where they spend 35 or more hours each week. They want to feel they have some control over their area, and rightly so. So there were compromises made by both management and staff, and to this day you will find things pinned or stuck on the partitions.

One way to alleviate this problem is to acquire partitions which have an area particularly constructed to serve as a bulletin board. It seems that in recent years the manufacturers of partitions have discovered that employees will always want to attach something to them, and so now they provide an area for doing this without actually affecting the partition surface itself.

Another consideration is the height of the partitions. They are available in several heights, the most common being four and six feet. In our situation higher partitions were allocated to managers and the Personnel Department, which required a certain amount of privacy. You will always find that people will stop and talk over the smaller partitions, and of course exceptionally tall people will be able to talk over the six foot high units. Attempts should be made to reduce this activity, but it will never be eliminated entirely.

Other problems will creep into the open office scenery. I can still see the six foot coat tree sticking up over the four foot partition and the photograph of a wife and children perched on the top ledge of a screen. One morning two plants appeared in the office. This normally would not be a problem, except in this case they were hanging by chains from the ceiling. It didn't do much for the appearance of the office, or for the staff who walked into them!

Disagreements over the office environment can also lead to serious personnel problems, as an experience I was involved in aptly demonstrates.

An Irate VP

Perhaps I had been somewhat lax in enforcing the rules regarding appearance, but it was a busy period and there were more important things to do. At that time there was a particular Vice-President who was known to have a "short fuse". The first indication of any problem was a loud screeching voice. As I left my office to see what was happening, I encountered a very unprofessional approach to management. The VP, in a voice which could be heard throughout the office was telling one of my clerks to "get that poster off the filing cabinet". He went on to state emphatically that the furniture was not to be used for everybody's pictures and posters. The young clerk was dismayed and angry, and I couldn't blame him. Even though he may have been right, the VP had made several mistakes:
• He should not have criticized a staff member in front of his peers.
• It was not his responsibility to deal with the problem, it was mine. He should have come to me and had me handle it.
• He should not have lost his temper.
What did all this accomplish? The VP looked bad in the eyes of the staff who now had very little respect for him. We also had a competent staff member who was angry and ready to quit. All because of a little piece of paper on a filing cabinet.

Other Amenities

Even in a small office the staff should have some place where they can relax and take a break away from their desks, apart from the washroom. Too many organizations plan their space but leave no place where staff can sit and enjoy their coffee or meals. If they do not leave the office they must sit at their desk. Every office should provide space for relaxation. With so many employees working on computer terminals, many organizations forbid employees from taking drinks to their desk. Spilled drinks can sure mess up a keyboard.

Air quality is another important ingredient. Not enough humidity, too much humidity. I have had staff complain that they never had headaches until they joined World Vision, and went on to blame the perceived poor air quality in their office area. They may have had a point, but the cause could never be determined.

The most important items to consider in your facilities are furniture, partitions, walls and other amenities that make staff comfortable. Every organization should provide a work environment where staff can be comfortable and productive.

How the office looks is important, but more important is how it feels!

Separated Operations

"Can we get this meeting started? Who are we waiting for?"

"We're waiting for John. He's on his way from the other office".

Does this sound familiar? I heard it often during one period when World Vision's Donor Development division was located in leased premises a few blocks away from the main building. It is never a good idea to split the operation's office facilities. Let's consider some of the problems.

• The separated group tends to become parochial. They develop a feeling of being isolated from the larger group. Problems can manifest themselves in various ways. Policies can easily be thwarted while the staff begins to plan their own activities such as picnics, etc. There develops a distinct feeling amongst the separated group that they are different, and in many instances they might seek to be treated differently by the organization.

• Lost productivity on the part of many staff. The time wasted in travelling between the offices for meetings is one example of this. I remember the many times I heard staff in the separated office say,

"It is really inconvenient to have to go to the National Office for meetings". As a result of that attitude, many times when people should have met, they did not.

• Communications are hindered. Sending documents between buildings is inconvenient and time consuming.

• Duplication of administrative costs. Consider the installation of another telephone system, computer cabling required to connect terminals to the main office, two postal addresses. The list goes on.

• Lack of contact with senior management. In one organization I asked staff in a separated location if the CEO had ever visited their offices. I was not surprised when they told me he had been there about a year ago. Most CEOs do not find the time to visit remote offices. They find time to walk around the main office and speak to staff, but seldom take time to visit staff in separated offices.

Organizations do not have separated operations by choice. It is usually forced on them by circumstances which could have been avoided with proper planning. If it is necessary to separate into two or more locations, make sure it is a temporary situation. One organization I know has operations in three locations and they are suffering because of it.

Appearance of Facilities

What is done with the type of facilities, space and furnishings and other things I have mentioned will be governed by available finances. An organization must live within its means. World Vision was able to purchase land in Mississauga and construct a 22,000 square foot building without appealing to its donors for funds. Income from estates along with bank financing provided the necessary funds to complete the project. Every charitable organization needs to consider the impact upon its budget when looking at space needs. But most, if not all, would hesitate to solicit funds from regular donors for 'bricks and mortar'. They could risk losing some of their funding for regular programs.

Donors can also react adversely to the type and size of the facility used by a charitable organization. Some will criticize any office which makes the organization look affluent. Be careful not to appear extravagant while realizing that most donors do not appreciate a facility that looks inefficient and cheap.

I am reminded of the story of the old accountant who, when he arrived at the office every day, would remove his coat, hang it on the coat tree and proceed to his old wooden desk and stool. He was a diligent worker. Hour after hour he would write up the accounts with his straight pen and nib, repeatedly dipping into the ink well. He had a green eye shade that kept the brightness of a 25 watt bulb out of his eyes. For years the office environment had been the same. Then one day he arrived and found that management had moved his desk to the other side of the office where the light was much better. He surveyed the situation and then proceeded to his boss's office. As he entered, the boss looked up and said, "I hope you like the new desk location. It should give you much better lighting for all of the detailed work that you do".

The accountant responded, "I quit", and walked out.

The boss was dumbfounded. He did not know that for all those years the accountant could only balance his books because he knew that the "debits were on the window side".

Never underestimate the value of the office environment.

9

Accountability: The Guilt Trip

"Answerable". This is one definition of the word accountable. We are all answerable to someone for something. It's a fact of life.

My first recollection of this principle came when I was in the first grade at school. Realizing that chewing gum in the classroom was not allowed, I removed the wad of gum from my mouth and placed it on the top of my desk for later use. Miss Armstrong (my favourite teacher) noticed the gum, had me dispose of it and chastened me for bringing it into the classroom. Not only that, I had to carry a "misconduct notice" to my mother and have her sign it before returning it to the teacher the next day. When I arrived home that afternoon, my mother was not there. Not knowing exactly how mother would react to this official notice from the teacher, I left the note on the table and went to bed. I awoke to the realization that I was answerable for my actions as it took only a few minutes for mother to administer the wooden brush following her short lecture.

Although I felt that the punishment outweighed the crime, there was no doubt in my mind that I was being held accountable for my actions.

Accountability does not only apply to people. Organizations are also accountable. Profit making companies are accountable to their shareholders, charitable organizations to their donors. In this chapter we will examine various areas of accountability.

ACCOUNTABILITY TO DONORS

The necessity for charities to provide information to their donors was recognized by the Canadian Institute of Chartered Accountants in a research study several years ago. It was found that since donors provide financial resources for non-profit organizations, they require information in order to make decisions regarding the extent and timing of future contributions. In other words, it is not likely that donors will continue to support a charity that does not provide information on how their donations are spent. The study went on to say that donors are interested in the nature of an organization's activities and its stewardship of resources. They are concerned with management's effective use of resources consistent with the organization's objectives.

ACCOUNTABILITY TO GOVERNMENT

Charitable organizations are not only accountable to their donors. They must also meet government regulations as well. Revenue Canada regulates the activities of charities in Canada, even though the provincial governments claim that they have jurisdiction over charities operating in their province. The federal government maintains the accountability of registered charities by requiring them to meet an annual disbursement quota and to file annual returns. Failure to meet these requirements may result in the revocation of a charity's registration allowing it to issue official donor receipts.

Provincial governments also exercise considerable control over charities and require a fair amount of accountability. In Ontario, for instance, this is accomplished through the office of the Public Trustee and the Charities Accounting Act, which gives the Public Trustee the responsibilities and powers of supervision over the administration of charitable trusts. This power includes visitation and examination of the state, management and condition of every charitable institution. Information required for submission to the Public Trustee includes a copy of the annual audited financial statements.

Where there is concern about the administration and management of a charity, the Public Trustee can require the charity to turn its accounts over to the Courts. In cases of misappropriation of funds or other serious mismanagement, the Public Trustee may apply to the Courts to have himself appointed Trustee over the charity, thus effectively taking control from the directors.

(Specific information on the Public Trustee's role within each province can be obtained through provincial government offices.)

ACCOUNTABILITY TO OTHER GROUPS

During the 1970's many religious organizations in the United States became concerned about a move towards increased government control over their activities. This resulted in the establishment of groups like The Evangelical Council for Financial Accountability (ECFA) in 1979. This particular organization developed standards to which their member organizations must adhere. These standards relate to such things as the Board of Directors, Audited Financial Statements, Audit Review Committee, Financial Disclosure, Integrity and Conflicts of Interest. Since 1987 guidelines have also been established for fund-raising, which covers areas such as Truthfulness in Communication, Communications and Donor Expectations, Communication and Donor Intent, Projects Unrelated to a Ministry's Primary Purpose, Incentive and Premiums, Reporting, Percentage Compensation for Fund-raisers, Tax Deductible Gifts for a Named Recipient's Personal Benefit, Conflict of Interest on Royalties, Acknowledgement of Gifts in Kind, Acting in the Interest of the Donor and Financial Advice.

It's obvious that they are serious about accountability.

In Canada, the Canadian Council Of Christian Charities (CCCC) also became concerned about standards of accountability for its member organizations. In 1981, as a member of the board and its Accountability Committee, I was involved in researching how the CCCC might introduce standards in Canada similar to those of the ECFA in the U.S.

The CCCC first looked at the possibility of having a Canadian ECFA. However, after meeting with ECFA it was decided that the CCCC should establish its own financial accountability standards and issue its own seal of approval.

When CCCC member organizations renewed their memberships in 1982 they were requested to voluntarily submit an audited financial statement. More than 50% of the organizations complied. This indicated that there was an interest in financial accountability. A very positive response to a survey of members confirmed this interest. In 1983 a number of organizations became charter members of the CCCC Seal for Financial Accountability. At the present time over 100 organizations have been approved to display the Seal and must adhere to several conditions:

1. The organization shall have an active responsible board, a majority of whom together are not employees or immediate family members. The board should meet at least twice yearly and have authority to set policy.

2. The organization shall have an annual audit by a public accountant.

3. The organization shall, upon request, make available its audited financial statements to anyone who requests them.

4. The organization shall have an active audit review committee.

5. The organization shall carry on its activities with the highest standards of integrity and avoid conflicts of interest.

6. The organization shall have a clearly defined statement of faith.

7. The organization shall in all of its programs and activities be consistent with its stated purposes and objectives. Donated funds shall be applied for the purposes for which they were received.

What benefits are provided to organizations that meet the financial standards?

(a) It indicates that the organization has a uniform accounting system consistent with good stewardship.

(b) It gives donors guidance in deciding what charities will receive their support.

(c) It builds credibility and confidence with a critical public.

(d) It indicates to regulatory bodies the seriousness with which CCCC regards financial accountability.

Not all member organizations of the CCCC have a need for this Seal of Financial Accountability. Smaller charities and those which do not raise funds from the public sector will not see the need for this public display of standard record keeping. This does not indicate that these charities are any less responsible in their financial accountability but it does mean that they are not reviewed annually by the CCCC Standards Committee. At the same time, a code of ethics is still in place to which all member organizations should adhere.

BETTER BUSINESS BUREAUS (BBB)

Friend or foe?

I had several encounters with the BBB during my years with World Vision. We sent an Annual Report and a copy of the audited financial statement to all BBB offices every year. I found that keeping their files up to date was much better than waiting until they requested information following an inquiry from some concerned donor.

On one occasion, we received a report from a donor in New Brunswick that he had received negative information about World Vision from the BBB office in Moncton. Consequently, he began to question whether he should continue to support the organization. Upon investigation I discovered that the files in the Moncton office contained information on World Vision in the U.S. which was not relevant to the operations of World Vision in Canada. This event prompted me to make sure that BBB offices across Canada were updated annually with information concerning the organization.

BBB offices in Canada see themselves as a watchdog over charities, protecting the public from fraudulent operations (which unfortunately do exist). In Toronto the BBB has a Philanthropic Advisory Service which publishes a pamphlet entitled "Give, But Give Wisely". This pamphlet provides information to donors on various charitable organizations which have been rated by the BBB.

In the Fall of 1989 the Toronto BBB established a Charitable Solicitations Review Board, on which I presently serve. This board rates Canadian charities and fund-raising organizations and provides this information to the public. This board is not intended to be judge and jury of Canadian charities. Charities for the most part are above reproach but the BBB strongly feels that the public should be able to get answers to their questions or concerns about charities and their fund-raising activities. This Review Board was established after a consumer survey indicated that eighty-seven percent of respondents favoured the creation of an independent panel to rate charities and fund-raising professionals.

It is a good practice for every charity to supply current information to BBB offices in Canada.

DONOR TREATMENT

An important consideration in financial accountability is the way in which charities relate to their donors. A donor will not continue to support an organization in which he has lost confidence. In dealing with donors, a charity should have two main goals – how to initiate confidence in donors to attract them, and how to maintain that confidence.

As noted earlier, one of the CCCC financial accountability standards requires that an organization provide an audited financial statement to anyone who requests it. There was a time when charities did not want to disclose too much information about their finances. My training as a Chartered Accountant convinced me of the need for confidentiality in all financial matters. Consequently, I was hesitant to send information on World Vision's finances to donors and I often wondered why they wanted it in the first place. I thought perhaps they would somehow use it against the organization. Although we had nothing to hide, my experience had affected my attitude towards disclosure. When I was involved in my own company, only my partner and I needed to see the financial statements. When I worked for Nestle, which was a private company, the financial statements went only to the head office in Switzerland. I was not comfortable giving out certain financial information.

During the past few years it has become routine to have charities release their financial statements to the public. In fact, I would not support a charity that wouldn't provide me with an audited financial statement upon request. Certainly, the recent public disclosure of the fraudulent actions within some well known charities has created some suspicion on the part of the donating public.

The media sometimes view themselves as the public protectors when it comes to charities. Most charitable organizations have nothing to hide, but they still live in the fear of some investigative reporter writing something derogatory about them. Unfortunately, in dealing with the media, once statements are made there is little you can do to have them corrected even if the information is not factual. Some charities are highly visible because of their size or high profile media promotions. These organizations tend to be more vulnerable to media attack.

A recent television show in Europe attacked the credibility of World Vision, resulting in a substantial decrease in donations. Although a successful slander suit was lodged against the producers of the show, the damage had already been done. The retraction never had the same impact as the damaging report.

Newspaper articles are often written about certain charities, arguing that too much money is spent on fund-raising and administration and not enough on charitable activities. This is one of the most popular areas of attack. A few years ago the Toronto Star featured an article about World Vision. Information that had been provided to the newspaper by one of the major Canadian church denominations was presented in such a way as to make it impossible to allow a fair comparison between their operations and World Vision's. Obviously, the intent was to make World Vision look bad because it was raising funds in the denomination's churches which officials felt should be directed to their own overseas programs. The newspaper compared the administration and fund raising costs of World Vision with those of the denomination. It was an unfair comparison because the denomination did not have to expend effort or funds to raise their dollars because they were collected through Sunday offerings. On the other hand World Vision had to pay promotional costs to raise the funds for its projects. Here again, the damage was irreparable because the readers would never hear about the incorrect information used in the report or of the meetings that took place between World Vision officials and the denomination's hierarchy after the newspaper article appeared.

All of this attention should make charities more aware of their vulnerability and give them reason to be careful about spending their donors' money. However, organizations should also be careful not to overreact. It is not necessary for the management and boards of charitable organizations to be paranoid about being investigated or being asked difficult questions. A careful review of their operations, followed by preparing responses to potential questions, should suffice. Of course, changes should be made that will make the organization more efficient, but major changes shouldn't be made solely because of the possibility of scrutiny by an outsider.

An annual audited report would be sufficient in most cases to satisfy financial questions from the public. But we must also be prepared for the more in depth questions about how the organization spends its money. But in doing so, caution should be exercised in order to ensure that donors and the media do not dictate how the organization should manage its affairs. Pleasing everybody is impossible but most people just want honest answers to their questions.

An example of this principle is World Vision's land purchase and office building construction several years ago. Donors were never asked to give funds to this project. Funding came from other sources, but this did not prevent criticism from those who saw the building as a waste of money. They did not like to see funds used to purchase bricks and mortar. Compared with the cost of continuing to lease space, however, there was no question that constructing a building was a more efficient and economical solution. Most donors reacted favourably when the reasoning behind the decision was given.

ONE POSITIVE REACTION

Over the years I have been asked many times by donors to disclose the salaries of World Vision management. As I stated previously, the giving of financial information was difficult for me. The disclosure of salary information was even more difficult. I asked myself, "Does a donor or a prospective donor have the right to know the salaries of senior management?" My policy has been to answer these questions by sending information on salary levels and how they were established. Very seldom was I required to give actual salary figures. But in some cases this did happen. This is a sensitive area and one which should be dealt with delicately.

On one occasion, a letter was received asking about the salary of the CEO. I had a standard response to these requests in which I quoted certain figures. In this particular case, my fears were unfounded about this information being published in some newspaper in Canada when I received, about a month later, a letter thanking me for the response and our willingness to be open about this matter. Enclosed was a cheque made out to World Vision in the amount of one thousand dollars. In this case, openness was rewarded. I can only expect that this will be the normal response when organizations become transparent to their donors.

Not all donor enquires are this encouraging. We have had letters asking questions such as: "What are the salaries of the 'big boys?'"; "What kind of house does the CEO live in, the number of rooms and its value?"; "What kind of car does the CEO drive?".

One day a call was received by World Vision from a prospective donor. He wanted to visit the office to find out more about the organization and its work. He arrived a few days later and spent some time with senior staff. After he left, the staff members remarked that they hoped he might send a donation or sponsor a child, but he had made no commitment. A few weeks later we received a letter from the gentleman who happened to live in British Columbia (we had not realized that he had flown to Toronto just to investigate the organization). The major surprise was a cheque he had enclosed for over $200,000. This was followed by further donations. In all, this man gave several hundred thousand dollars to the organization. His trust in the organization was established during his visit to the office where we were able to "be transparent".

We need to remember that donors have the right to ask questions about how a charity uses their money. The charity in all respects should be transparent, especially in the financial areas. The fear of damaging the organization's reputation is not a good reason to withhold information from enquirers.

10

Auditors, Lawyers and Consultants – Heads You Win, Tails You Lose

I'm tempted to say something humorous about these three professions, but there is nothing funny about auditors, lawyers or consultants! I have been an auditor, and a consultant, never a lawyer. God has been good to me in this respect.

Every charitable organization will require the services of one or more of these professionals at some time or another and would be foolish not to have such counsel available. Consultants are being used more by charitable organizations today than ever before, especially within specialized areas such as computer technology.

This chapter will look at various issues concerning the services offered by these professionals and when to use them.

AUDITORS

Mrs. Smith had worked for the company for many years and was nearing retirement. I don't think her job had changed since the day she started. She was a permanent fixture in the Accounts Receivable Department.

It was my first visit to this particular company, so I had never met Mrs. Smith. As part of my review, I had to obtain the sales records from her and do some verification of the accounts receivable balances. I very professionally and kindly approached her and asked if I might have her records for review. Her response surprised me. "Why do you want to look at my records? Doesn't the company trust me? I've worked here all these years and never had anyone ask to see my work. Is that all you auditors do; come and look for other people's mistakes"?

With that, she proceeded to show me where the records were located. As I walked away with the books under my arm, I glanced back and saw her sitting at her desk shaking her head in obvious disappointment at the way the company and the auditors were treating her. After all, she was one of their most loyal employees.

This event occurred early on in my auditing career while I was an apprentice. For some time after that, I had the distinct impression that our clients' employees all felt the same way about me. I was only there to find their errors. In fact, auditors were looked upon by many people in those days as investigators looking for employees who were stealing from the company. (We did find some.)

But times have changed. Professional accountants now serve their clients in many different capacities, offering such services as financial planning and tax advice. Many of the large accounting firms also provide consulting services.

Still, many managers's and board member's first encounter with an auditor is during a year end audit.

Do We Need An Audit?

Canadian charities in most instances are not required by law to have a professional audit. Many smaller charities only produce unaudited annual financial statements. The Canadian Institute Of Chartered Accountants has established standards for both audit and review engagements. A review is different from an audit in that the scope of a review is less than that of an audit and therefore the level of assurance provided by a review is lower. A review consists primarily of inquiries, analytical procedures and discussion related to information supplied to the public accountant by the organization with the limited objective of assessing whether the information being reported on is plausible within the framework of appropriate criteria. A review does not require the public accountant to seek supporting or independent evidence or to study and evaluate internal controls. The lower cost of the review engagement is an important consideration.

For smaller charities this may be an acceptable approach. But for the larger more public charities, it could pose some problems, particularly in the area of donor acceptance. There is not only an advantage to having the name of a firm of Chartered Accountants (CA) on the organization's annual financial report, but in the case of very large and public charities it is a distinct advantage to have one of the larger, well known firms performing the audit.

While the cost of having a CA perform the audit must be weighed by smaller charities, there is a size at which every charitable organization should consider such an audit. But size and cost should not be the only considerations in making this decision. Other factors might include:

• a change in CEO, where he and/or the board may request that an audit be performed to verify that the accounts are in order at the time of the change
• the organization is facing financial difficulties
• requests by a third party such as a bank when the organization wants to borrow funds
• the board is suspicious that the assets are being misappropriated
• requests from government agencies such as the Canadian International Development Agency, if the organization is receiving grants
• at the request of the Treasurer of the board of smaller charities where he is responsible for the preparation of financial statements.
• a requirement of the Canadian Council of Christian Charities in order to obtain their Seal of Financial Accountability.

These are some of the reasons that should be considered by every charity when engaging a professional accountant to perform an audit.

Who Are The Professional Accountants?

I have been making one major assumption in the area of professional accountants, and that is that they would be Chartered Accountants. This does not preclude the fact that there are professional accountants with other qualifications who perform audits and provide other professional services. These would include Certified General Accountants and Certified Management Accountants. However, being a CA, I do have somewhat of a bias. My comments are not meant to demean the other accounting professions, but only to explain that there is a difference in the level of professional training. Some may disagree with this opinion.

One major event that influenced my opinion occurred while I was studying to be a CA and working for student wages in a CA firm. I was in the third year of my five year course of study when it was announced that as a result of a merger, Certified Public Accountants (CPAs) would become CAs. My reaction was not unlike most of the other students. CPAs had received their designations through study, but with one major difference. They had not been required to work for an accounting firm and therefore had the privilege of earning higher wages while studying. Also, they had not had the auditing experience which was provided through employment with CA firms. Perhaps a moot point but one that was upsetting to many of the CA students at that time.

The events surrounding that merger clarified for many CAs and others in the business community and government that CA standards were higher than those set by other accounting bodies in Canada. In my estimation that has not changed. In fact, a recent survey of Chief Financial Officers and controllers of large companies in Ottawa on the importance of education to business success, indicated that 65% of the respondents would look for a CA if they were hiring a Chief Financial Officer. This was founded on the belief that a chartered accounting background provides a broader exposure and educational base, making the candidate more innovative.

Despite my bias, there is no reason that organizations should not have audits performed by other professional accountants. I just think that there is more depth of experience with a CA.

Other Services Provided By CAs

It is not my intention to list all of the services provided by Chartered Accountants. Details of these services can be obtained from materials published by most major accounting firms. However, there are specific areas that I have encountered in my years in management where I have looked to them for assistance.

They can be very helpful in the preparation of financial information, whether it be financial statements or other special reports required by third parties. I have used this type of assistance many times, especially when the organization wanted to add credibility to a report. Having a CA's name on a report adds a distinct measure of acceptance for the reader.

Some smaller charities have a CA prepare monthly financial statements and review them with management. This service is usually provided for organizations that do not have a full time accountant or employ a bookkeeper who isn't qualified to prepare financial statements. Some organizations also engage a CA to prepare reports or forms required by government agencies.

A CA can be very helpful in preparing cash flow projections for major projects that the organization is planning, such as a new building or any major purchase.

Advice on accounting matters that pertain to charitable organizations is something that most CAs can offer. The CA profession operates under guidelines which are contained in the Canadian Institute of Chartered Accountants Handbook. The handbook lists the auditing and accounting standards pertaining to not-for-profit organizations. If your organization is working with a CA, these standards will be used in the audit of your organization, and the accounting standards will govern how the auditor comments on your financial statements.

It Can Be Costly

There are many ways in which a CA can assist your organization, but there is something else to consider – the cost! CAs are professionals, and they charge professional fees at professional rates. Every time the organization uses the services of the CA, it must be prepared to pay the cost. Every organization must give consideration at some time in its growth on whether it is more cost effective to employ someone with professional accounting skills, rather than pay the costs of periodically engaging someone to perform specific tasks.

It may not be necessary to hire a CA or someone that has an accounting degree, but the organization needs to be very careful about employing someone with the required level of expertise. I know of a charitable organization that does not have the personnel required to prepare year-end schedules for the auditors. As a result, the auditors spend days preparing these schedules, with a resulting fee increase of several thousand dollars. The obvious recommendation to management is for them to acquire the additional staff that can do this work. It would probably be more economical for the organization to pay a salary than to run up audit fees.

Most of the major CA firms provide audit fee discounts to not-for-profit clients. This amount can vary but can be as high as 25%. Fees for special services are usually charged at the going rate.

The Appointment

The Board of Directors (or the Corporation members, depending on the structure) appoint the auditors, usually at the annual meeting. This means that the auditors are ultimately responsible to the board, not management. The board engages them, sets the fee, and removes them if necessary.

In my estimation, any board would be foolish to appoint auditors without first discussing the appointment with management. Although the auditors are the board's responsibility, the CEO and the Chief Financial Officer are the ones who will have the most contact with them.

Some religious organizations are concerned whether the auditor should be someone with similar religious beliefs. While this shouldn't be a necessary prerequisite, it would be an advantage if the auditor had a special understanding of the ethos and key objective of the organization. However, CAs with the same religious leanings do not necessarily have the best available knowledge and abilities to meet the organization's needs. As a Christian, I view Christian CAs the same way I view Christian plumbers. I like to hire the best, but you don't have to be a Christian to be proficient. That's why I do not support the publication of Christian yellow pages that have appeared in some parts of North America. The organization's needs should be paramount in any decision. Religious organizations should not be obsessed with engaging only religious CAs. I would certainly look for a CA that would understand and be sympathetic to the work of the organization, but not at the risk of the organization failing to receive the level of service it requires.

Auditors should not be appointed for life. Every three years (five at the most) consideration should be given to putting the audit out to tender. World Vision Canada did this a few years ago, having had the same auditors for over 15 years. There had been changes in their staff and partners over those years, but nothing major had occurred to cause the board or management to review the relationship. Then the supervision of the audit was moved to a new office and new partners were assigned the work. This did not create any problems at first, but for various reasons tensions arose in the relationship. Both management and the board then decided that the audit should be tendered. Three other firms, including the incumbent, were invited to tender. As a result of this exercise, new auditors were appointed for a term of three years with a substantial fee reduction.

Several questions should be asked each year about the auditor's performance.

• Are they meeting the expectations of the board and management?
• Is the audit cost reasonable?
• Are the auditors able to provide the level of service required? This especially pertains to organizations that have possibly outgrown their auditor.

If there are any concerns about the present auditor's performance or fees, the Treasurer should meet with him and discuss the board's concerns. It is usually in the best interests of the organization to retain its present auditor. Cost is not the most important factor. The relationship that is built between an organization and its auditor cannot be overlooked. It takes years to develop this relationship and this should be considered in any move to replace your auditor.

LAWYERS

Some of my best friends are lawyers. Especially the ones who have defended me. In 1984 Revenue Canada decided to disallow my claim for housing allowance. For tax purposes, World Vision, my employer at that time, was classified as a "religious order". Because of my position within the organization I was able to claim a housing allowance and had done so for several years. But in this particular year a Revenue Canada clerk decided that I was not entitled to this claim and disallowed it. I filed a Notice Of Objection within the 90 day limit. The fight was on! It was almost five years later that Revenue Canada finally agreed to allow the claim.

A successful appeal would not have been possible without the involvement of a very knowledgable tax lawyer. He led me through the whole process and defended my position before the government. At one point I was required to sit through an Examination For Discovery with two lawyers from the Department of Justice. It would have been very difficult to face that inquisition without my lawyer. Through this experience I gained new insights into the value of not only having a lawyer but having the right lawyer.

There is not much I can say about lawyers that has not already been said. There is no doubt, I am sure, in anyone's mind that every organization needs legal counsel at one time or another. If your organization is trying to get by without legal advice it is treading on thin ice.

Do you need the services of a lawyer to register a charity with Revenue Canada? Not necessarily. Also, organizations can be incorporated in Canada without legal counsel. A charity doesn't need to be incorporated to be registered as a charity with Revenue Canada. Management must decide when to seek legal advice on these matters. It is prudent to have a lawyer involved if there are any peculiarities in the organizational structure.

Many charities attempt to have a lawyer on their board. This is very helpful but there are too many charities and too few lawyers.

The smaller charity will find that a lawyer with a smaller practice can provide the required services. However, as the organization grows, its legal requirements also grow. I have found that some organizations have outgrown their lawyer. Most lawyers in a small practice will refer any special needs to a larger practice. In World Vision we worked for many years with one lawyer who had his own practice. As the organization grew and relocated in another part of the city, it became difficult to have this lawyer handle every matter because of the growing complexity of the organization. It was also inconvenient to meet with a lawyer now located many miles from our office so I began to engage other lawyers depending on our particular needs.

Frequently, documents needed to be notarized. A lawyer, whose office was within walking distance of the office was retained to assist in some of our minor needs. When we were having problems with the Human Rights Commission, I sought out a lawyer in a large Toronto firm who specialized in labour law.

The acquisition of a major piece of property in Toronto was handled by another large legal firm who had the required specialists. Using a large firm is recommended, especially when the organization's needs become more complex. This same firm handled several issues – changes in letters patent, incorporating a new charity, settlement of a labour dispute, among others.

Is the board or management responsible for engaging the lawyer? I would like to think that legal matters pertaining to operations are the responsibility of management while corporate matters are a board responsibility. I had freedom to engage legal counsel whenever the need arose. Of course, I had to report regularly on the cost of legal fees, and it was company policy that nobody engaged legal counsel other than myself, the CEO or the board. Unfortunately, other staff sometimes would unwittingly approach a lawyer without my knowledge and I would only discover this when the invoice was received. In any organization, someone should be responsible for contact with legal counsel. This is usually the CEO or someone else in senior management.

Retaining legal counsel is a necessity in every organization. Because of the costs involved, however, it must be closely controlled.

CONSULTANTS

What is a consultant? I have been told that it's someone who can't find a full time job.

However, there are times when an organization should consider using a consultant. In charities with which I am familiar they are often used in such areas as data processing, fund raising, and general management. It is one way to obtain the expertise you require without hiring new staff. While it may be more expensive in per-hour costs, the consultant can be engaged for a specific project, for a specific length of time, and for a contracted price.

One word of caution. Sometimes current staff members also want to be consultants for the organization. You may have had that proposition made to you: "I've started my own company. Is it alright if I invoice the organization for the work I am doing and you can take me off the payroll"?

Be careful about engaging existing staff members as consultants and having them invoice you. Revenue Canada is very clear in its guidelines regarding employee/employer relationships. If the employee reports to work at the organization's office every day, and the employer has control over his time, then you probably have an employer/employee relationship. He must be paid in the regular manner and have the regular statutory deductions made from his wages. I have found that most people making approaches to their employers about billing as a consultant are trying to reduce their income tax liability. Also, a consultant should be able to show that he is working for several clients. Most full time staff may have difficulty proving this to the tax authorities.

According to Revenue Canada, a person is also considered an employee if they:

• work in one office a set number of hours per day

• must account to the company for time
• are frequently given instructions regarding the job
• receive group insurance and company pension benefits
• work in an office provided by the company along with necessary equipment to perform the tasks.

Conversely, consultant status would be more likely if:
• work is performed on a project basis with no commitment to regular hours each day
• work is performed without direct supervision
• the consultant invoices the company for work performed
• no employee benefits are provided
• the consultant uses his own equipment and works outside company premises.

Calling yourself a consultant does not necessary make you one in the eyes of Revenue Canada.

When you engage a consultant, make sure there is a clear and concise contract. If the amount of money involved is substantial, I would have legal counsel review it before signing.

If you are considering using consultants, make sure the organization budgets for them. In some situations the board has been surprised at the costs for consulting, especially if they were unaware of the extent consultants were being used. If the board is pressing management to keep salary costs to a minimum, management may turn to consultants as an alternative. However, the overall impact may be more costly. There is a place for consultants in charitable organizations, but not as a means of satisfying board demands for lower salaries.

In summary, remember that professional fees paid to accountants, lawyers and consultants should be budgeted for the year, using the best possible projections. Management should control the use of professionals and keep the board informed about which professionals are being engaged.

11

Bean Counting –
Always Necessary
Sometimes Fun

My wife can never balance her bank book. Every month when the bank statement arrives she compares their balance with hers and then proceeds to change her balance to agree with the bank. She disregards the possibility that some cheques have not yet cleared the bank account or her records do not include all of the bank charges. The important thing is to begin each month with the same figures as the bank. This is creative accounting. My wife is not an accountant and does not want to be one, although she is not as bad as the woman who told her husband she must have money in the bank because she still had blank cheques left in her purse!

Unfortunately, too many people approach financial questions in this manner. Although they can't be expected to understand the intricacies involved in accounting, they make decisions without ever considering basic financial principles. While these decisions frequently cause havoc in many households they also cause a lot of grief for charities.

World Vision has a number of donors who give substantial amounts of money each year. One such donor from Western Canada notified us that he was no longer going to be assisting the organization because of the amount spent on overhead expenses. He was not pleased about the percentage of his donations that were being spent on administration and fund raising costs.

As is usual in cases like this, we had our Western representative visit the donor to determine the extent of the problem and to provide an explanation of our finances with the goal of retaining his support. This was unsuccessful, so I flew to Vancouver to meet with the gentleman to explain how our finances were handled.

For two hours we reviewed current financial statements. I explained how figures were derived and how the organization designated their donations. As the time slipped by I felt that I was losing this donor. Nothing I said seemed to satisfy him in regards to how we were spending his contributions. Knowing that he was about to leave the meeting, I looked at the representative and then I looked at the donor and said, "If you feel you can no longer give to the organization, let me thank you for your support over the past few years. It has meant much to us".

As we were about to leave, I glanced down again at the financial statements and noticed the figure on the Income Statement under the Undesignated category. I turned the statement around so that the donor could see it and said, "By the way, did your realize that many donors give undesignated funds to the organization to be used for paying administrative and other non-program costs? In fact, last year that amounted to over a million dollars". He responded, "You mean you are not using 20% of my donations to pay your bills in Canada?"

This further explanation of World Vision's finances resulted in the donor continuing his support. Not only did we need to be transparent in this case but we had to adequately explain how funds were handled.

Too many charitable organizations do not maintain proper financial records. Accounting within charities requires some imagination and creativity, not to be devious but to simplify the tracking of donations, especially those designated for special projects.

At the present time there are few formal accounting standards governing charities in Canada. The accounting treatment of expenses in particular is very subjective, resulting in extreme difficulty when attempting to compare the financial reports of different charitable organizations.

CANADIAN INSTITUTE OF
CHARTERED ACCOUNTANTS

In 1980 a research study was published by the Canadian Institute of Chartered Accountants (CICA). The study was initiated because of the absence of appropriate reporting principles and standards for non-profit organizations. As a result, there was confusion and misunderstanding on the part of donors and other interested bodies. Understanding was hampered by the lack of uniformity in financial statements and in the degree of financial disclosure. Different terminology and accounting methods and uncertainty over what accounting principles should apply, also made comparison of financial reports difficult if not meaningless.

The CICA study did not result in any major changes to rectify the existing problems. But the CICA Handbook, Section 4230, now details how to account for certain matters that pertain to non-profit organizations. These include such things as: accrual accounting, the donation of fixed assets and services, pledges etc. For instance, CICA suggests that financial statements should be prepared on an accrual basis.

On the matter of accounting for pledges, CICA recommends:

• "The policy followed in accounting for pledges should be disclosed".

• "When pledges are recorded, the amount recorded should be disclosed".

• "Pledges normally do not represent legally enforceable claims against the donors. However, pledges can have a significant impact on the financial condition and operating results of non-profit organizations. An organization may choose to record the value of pledges, but would do so only when a realizable value can be reasonably estimated. Disclosure of the realizable value of pledges not recorded is desirable, if such value can be reasonably estimated".

On the matter of fixed assets CICA suggests:

• "The policy followed in accounting for fixed assets should be disclosed. Where fixed assets are expensed immediately, the amount expensed should be disclosed".

• "Methods used by non-profit organizations to account for fixed assets include: (a) capitalize and depreciate; (b) capitalize but do not depreciate, and; (c) expense immediately".

• "Variations of these methods are also used. An organization may

use the same method for all its fixed assets or different methods may
be used for different types of assets".

• "Pending completion of a current project on fixed assets, and an
evaluation of the appropriateness of the methods used by non-profit
organizations, the Committee is not making recommendations for
accounting measurement of fixed assets for non-profit organizations".

These are just some samples of how CICA views the treatment of
certain financial matters affecting non-profit organizations, but much
more needs to be done in this whole area.

However, expenses still do not have generally accepted accounting
principles applied to them. Recently, CICA's Accounting Standards
Committee completed its latest research aimed at bringing more accounting applications for non-profit organizations into the Handbook.
It has revised and expanded Section 1000, "Financial Statement Con-
cepts", to outline principles that apply specifically to the non-profit
sector. Also, a CICA task force on non-profit organizations is cur-
rently developing accounting recommendations specifically in five
general areas – capital assets and depreciation, financial statement
presentation, fund accounting reporting issues, defining the reporting
entity, and revenue and capital considerations.

OTHER ATTEMPTS AT SETTING GUIDELINES

Another attempt to develop guidelines for certain financial transac-
tions within non-profit organizations was made by a group called the
Evangelical Joint Accounting Committee. Established in the United
States, it included representation from the following groups:

• Christian Ministries Management Association
• Evangelical Council For Financial Accountability
• Evangelical Foreign Mission Association
• Interdenominational Foreign Mission Association

The committee's work included the publishing of an Accounting
And Financial Reporting Guide in 1987. The purpose of the publication was to attain the maximum degree of uniformity in accounting
and financial reporting among organizations associated with the
member groups, while adhering to generally accepted accounting
principles. Members of the committee included chief financial officers
from major charities, public accounting practitioners, professional
consultants, and representatives from the sponsoring agencies.

ALLOCATION OF EXPENSES

Charitable organizations are continually being asked to justify their overheads, which represents money that the organization spends on itself as opposed to money spent on its programs. Most commonly, these can be categorized as **Administration Costs** and **Fund Raising Costs.** Any funds not spent in these categories are usually determined to be **Program Costs.** Fixed assets costs are usually capitalized and the write off for depreciation becomes an administration cost. How do charities determine what expenses should go into each of these categories? Who sets the guidelines?

In non-profit organizations this is one of the most important aspects of financial presentations, and it is also one of the most difficult to determine. In 1983 World Vision Canada examined this issue and finally produced some guidelines which attempted to provide a rationale that was consistent with the existing definitions and standards set by the Interdenominational Foreign Mission Association (IFMA) and that were in keeping with generally accepted accounting standards. The IFMA has existed since 1917 and assists organizations in demonstrating accountability for the funds they receive while practising full financial disclosure. This organization has very high standards which have gained for it and its members a reputation of proven excellence and integrity.

Any approach to full accountability requires that definitions be determined for the major cost areas within charities – Program, Fund Raising and Administration.

Although any approach to defining these cost areas will be subjective and may vary considerably from one organization to another, some commonality will prevail. Let's take a look at these most critical cost areas, and try to define them.

Program Costs

This category would normally include the activities performed by the organization that are directly related to accomplishing its charitable goals as set out by its key objective. In other words, these costs should in no way be related to fund raising or administration. They would be the costs directly related to carrying out programs. One example might be the cost of purchasing food for hungry people. The programs of the charity can usually be easily identified. Costs that can properly be identified as necessary to the actual carrying out of these programs should be allocated to the Program area.

Fund Raising Costs

These expenses are incurred in inducing others to contribute money, securities, time, materials or facilities for which the contributor will not receive a direct economic benefit. Some questions need to be asked, however. For instance, are staff who answer donors' telephone enquiries fund raisers or administrative staff? Is the monthly magazine which contains articles about the work of the organization a fund raising activity? If we accept that the production of receipts is an administrative cost, does part of this cost become fund raising if a donation request is printed on it? You can see that there are numerous factors to consider.

Administration Costs

Expenses in this category include costs related to the overall direction of the organization's affairs as contrasted with expenses incurred for specific program or fund raising activities. In my experience these expenses include the expenses of the Accounting Department, costs related to facilities, the Personnel Department and computer activities.

Every charity needs to review how it categorizes is expenses. This is not only important for conveying accurate information to donors and government agencies, but it is important to management in controlling finances.

HOW TO BEGIN

Review all cost items and determine the categories to which they belong. A number of these costs will fall into more than one category. A determination will have to be made as to what percentage should be allocated to each category. For example, when the CEO travels overseas to visit projects, is this a program cost or an administrative cost? An accurate analysis of the activity will help to determine the allocation for each of the two categories. If the trip was also made to provide film or support for promotional activities, then some of the cost would fall under fund raising.

The important thing is to review every expense item and categorize it. Again, the outcome of this type of study will differ for each organization. The importance of this exercise is to develop guidelines that will assist in preparing accurate financial figures that can be used in response to questions from donors and the media.

Once you have established a rationale for the allocation of expenses, have your auditors review it. The board of directors should approve the rationale and include it in the policy and procedure manual. Now the organization has some justification for the manner in which it classifies its expenses. It may be questioned by others, but it is a basis from which to respond to questions.

The allocation rationale should be reviewed annually and commented upon by the auditors as to its consistency of application. Once such a policy is in place it will provide a guideline for cost allocation when new programs are implemented or new and different types of expenses occur.

FUND RAISING AND ADMINISTRATION –
HOW MUCH IS REASONABLE?

Some donors always think too much money is used for fund raising and administration costs. They will decide what is acceptable for your organization and if they feel that these costs are too high they will not support the charity. The media, who sometimes see themselves as "protectors of the donors", will also try to determine what is a reasonable level of spending for fund raising and administration. Revenue Canada also sets guidelines in its Disbursement Quota regulation.

This requires that every year a charity must spend on its charitable activities an amount equal to its disbursement quota for the year. The quota is calculated at 80% of the gifts (donations) received by the organization in the preceding year for which it issued official tax receipts.

Fund raising and administration costs are necessary to the efficient operation of any charity. Without an investment in fund raising activities, the organization would never grow and would not be able to expand its charitable activities. In fact, if new donors are not found, the organization would eventually become extinct. I have never excused the need to spend money to raise money. The problem is maintaining an acceptable level.

In my experience, ensuring that fund raising and administration costs do not exceed twenty percent of income is reasonable (10% on fund raising and 10% on administration). Although the percentages will vary from charity to charity, people tend to make comparisons without taking into account the various types of charities and their activities. Some charities will, by their very nature, have a higher level of supporting costs than others.

Unfair Comparison

Lou worked for me when I owned a catering company. He loved people and was always ready to help out in a time of need. Most Sundays found him in church and on many occasions he assisted in taking up the offering during the service. As he told it, he felt that most of the congregation needed to be motivated to give and to give generously, so just as he started the offering plate down the row he would place a $20 bill in it. The affect was always the same. People would see the large bill and give accordingly. He said it worked every time. What the people didn't know was that Lou removed the $20 bill from the plate when it came back to him. Now that's fund raising with very little cost!

If you were to compare the costs of a church operated charity with a charity that must raise its support from the public at large, you would find a big difference in costs. Fund raising costs of a publicly supported charity are necessarily higher because funds for a church operated charity come directly from its various congregations. To arrive at a fair comparison you would have to take into account the operating costs of various churches. To compare the fund raising and administration costs of the United Way with those of the Salvation Army would be impractical.

Another reason why cost comparisons are difficult stems from a lack of standards in the area of accounting for costs. Unless every charity classifies its spending into cost centres based on some standard that applies to all, there will always be a disparity.

The quality of the charitable activities and the accomplishments of the organization will also reflect on its spending ratios. Some charities may be quite content to operate out of a warehouse, working on orange crates so that more of its money can be spent on programs. This may look good on the financial statements, but its overall objectives may not be met as a result. The quality of any organization is usually a reflection of how well it is administered. Poor administration usually results in poor quality programs.

What Does The Donor Expect?

I think donors expect the organization to be efficient in all areas. If the organization is spending wisely and is efficient, most donors will accept a reasonable level of administration and fund raising costs. If you can invite the donor to your office and feel comfortable with its appearance and have no difficulty explaining how you are spending his money, you will have a happy supporter.

A level of transparency in fund raising and administration costs must be maintained. These are necessary expenses so make sure your donors understand them. Answer their questions honestly and without hesitation. Every donor expects and should receive this treatment.

Do not justify your fund raising and administration costs by comparing them with other organizations. I am a firm believer that you should never sell your product by running down the competition. Standing alone, any charity should be worthy of support based on its own performance and how it spends the money entrusted to it.

To summarize, it is important to establish proper accounting standards for your organization and to maintain them with consistency. Have your auditors review these standards and comment on them. Share the standards with your donors. Be transparent. Your donors will appreciate it.

Conclusion

"Old accountants never die, they just lose their balance".

Some people thought that this was my problem when I decided to resign from World Vision Canada in February 1990. Because this is a book about my experiences in management over the past 25 years, it seems appropriate that I conclude with some comments about the present.

I remained with World Vision Canada until June 1990. That summer was spent in Europe working as a consultant to another World Vision office, after which I returned to Canada to establish my own consulting and public accounting practice.

THE PAST

There is no better teacher than experience. The older you get, the more you know, and the more proficient you should be as a manager. The way that I manage now is a far cry from the way I managed in 1964. Much of my "education" has come from having mentors and a desire to learn from those who had valuable experiences to share.

Leo was a very quiet, unassuming man, who over my first five years in business would share with me his many years of management experience – successes and failures, workable and unworkable ideas, how to develop people skills and negotiating skills and so on. I was to learn things that you couldn't get from a textbook or a seminar. This dear man, who was my boss at the time, was able to share his business life with me. I soaked it up like a sponge.

There is a proverb that says, "Wisdom is supreme; therefore get wisdom. Though it cost all you have, get understanding". What a wonderful, basic truth! You may not have much of a past yet, or you may have plenty. What have your learned from your past? Who have you learned from? What have you learned that will make you a better manager? And are you using what you have learned?

There are many people from my past that have contributed to my development as a manger. When I was in the catering business, it was Leo. At Nestle, is was Roy and Dave. During my fifteen years with World Vision, I learned management skills from people like Bill Newell, Don Scott, Ted Engstrom, Ed Dayton and others. Working with experienced people is one of the best ways to prepare for a management role. Are there such people in your experience?

"Put It In Your Desk Until Tomorrow"

Another important lesson gained during my first few years in business was also taught to me by Leo. Angry with a client, I had written a fairly scathing letter, venting my frustrations. Presenting it to Leo to review before it was mailed, he handed it back to me and calmly said, "Put it in your desk until tomorrow". This was not what I had expected. I was angry. I had written exactly what I wanted to say and expressed exactly how I felt and wanted to get this note to the offending party as quickly as possible. But I took Leo's advice and placed the letter in the top drawer of my desk. The next morning I had forgotten that it was there. When I discovered it sometime later, I read it and promptly threw it into the wastebasket, saying to myself, "How could you have written such a letter?" This was not me!

Since that experience I have learned that it is okay to write a letter in anger but it is even more important to file the letter until the next day. This technique has saved me untold embarrassment and enabled me to retain valuable relationships. This experience has remained with me over the years and has assisted me greatly in making management decisions.

But the past is past. We can never go back. If no one has assisted you in learning how to manage and you are in a management role, then you are experiencing "on the job training". This is not the best way to learn how to manage, and it certainly can be a source of frustration for those who work for you. However, in some organizations this is the only way they can develop management staff.

Whatever your situation, the question is not how well you managed in the past, or even how you perform as a manager at present. The important thing that you should be asking yourself is, "What can I do to make myself a better manager in the future?"

THE FUTURE

You are off to a good start – you have read this book!

The following suggestions will contribute to your success in management.

1. Find a Mentor

There are many good people in management who would gladly share from their experience. If these people cannot be found in your organization, look elsewhere.

2. Read, Read, Read

Read books on management. Arrange to receive a few good management newsletters.

3. Attend Seminars

Many management professionals offer valuable and practical seminars. Be selective. Review the presenters' qualifications and experience. (I still have a problem with unmarried people giving marriage seminars). A day or two away from the office is a profitable investment of time. I know many people who have attended seminars and tell me that the most valuable lessons were gained from talking with others with similar problems.

4. Take Some Management Courses

Most organizations will subsidize the cost of further education for staff. There are also many good management courses offered through universities and community colleges.

5. Join A Group

Join with a group of managers who meet periodically. Develop a relationship with people in management outside your own organization. This provides an opportunity to share ideas at meetings, over the telephone or at lunch.

6. Listen to Others

Too many of us think we know all of the answers, especially as we grow older. If you think you have "arrived", then perhaps it's time to retire. Listen to others in management. They may have discovered something that you don't know – a better way perhaps, or even a more cost effective method to accomplish certain tasks. Always be willing to listen and not just to managers. I have learned a great deal about managing people from the people I have managed. Don't ever stop listening to others and seek advice from those in whom you have confidence.

7. Accept Responsibility When Offered

Many good people who should be managers, are not. (Conversely, many people who are managing, should not be). Potential managers often refuse promotion because they fear they might fail. They do not want the responsibility that goes with managing: planning, organizing, leading, delegating, meeting report deadlines, resolving staff conflicts, disciplining, etc. If you are one of these people, I would encourage you to give yourself a chance to succeed. When the opportunity is offered for you to take on management responsibilities, it is usually because your superiors see some leadership potential in you. Quite often we fail to see this potential in ourselves.

8. Value People

This is probably the most important aspect to being a successful manager. Throughout this book I have stressed the value of people. If you do not know how to handle people, especially those who work directly under you, all your other management skills are useless. If you cannot build a strong supportive team that respects you and wants to work for you, you will never be completely fulfilled or successful as a manager.

There are people in senior management without people skills who usually reach their position by climbing over others. The organizations they work for are usually more concerned about their income than their people. In my estimation these managers are not successful.

The most important thing to remember is,

THE KEY TO SUCCESSFUL MANAGING IS TO SUCCESSFULLY MANAGE PEOPLE.

TO ORDER EXTRA COPIES
OF THIS BOOK

Copies of *What Are You Doing With My Money?* may be obtained by sending the form below, or a photocopy, to:

Ken Dick Management Consultants
P.O. Box 202
Streetsville, Ontario
L5M 2B8

Please enclose a cheque or money order for $12.95, plus taxes, and $1.50 for postage and handling PER BOOK.

Please send me _____ copies of *What Are You Doing With My Money?*

_____   Books at $12.95 each   _____

              GST (7% in Canada only)   _____

              Shipping and Handling
              ($1.50 per book)   _____

              **TOTAL PAYMENT
              ENCLOSED**   _____

Name _____

Address _____

_____

City _____

Province _____ Postal Code _____

Bulk Order Discounts: 10-24 books (10% discount), over 25 books (20% discount). Discount on book price only, not on postage.

Ken Dick is available for speaking engagements and provides consulting services to non-profit organizations.

For further information please write: Ken Dick Management Consultants, P.O. Box 202, Streetsville, Ontario, L5M 2B8.